Diary of a
DARTMOOR WALKER

conceived, compiled and written by
Chips Barber

amended, edited and refined by
Sally Barber

charted, cartographed and diagrammatised by
Dave Whalley

drawn, sketched and portrayed by
Jane Reynolds

OBELISK PUBLICATIONS

Other books by the Author:
Around and About the Haldon Hills
The Lost City of Exeter

This book is dedicated to: Theo, Dave C, Willy, Fingers, Bone, Mike, Clive, Dennis, Terry, Tom and Harold . . . old Uncle Tom Cobley and all!

PLATE ACKNOWLEDGEMENTS
Dave Whalley for all maps, profiles and cross sections
Jane Reynolds for all drawings
Mr Jones for the cover photo of a Roos Tor sunset and for page 109
Dave Coombs for page 117
Paul Williams for pages 32, 68
Mr Phillips for page 31
Mr Youngson for pages 97, 98
Mr Kneeshaw for page 30
All other photographs by Chips Barber

*First published in 1983
by Obelisk Publications,
22 Causey Gardens, Pinhoe, Exeter, Devon.
Designed, typeset and printed in Great Britain by
Penwell Ltd., Parkwood, Callington,
Cornwall.*

ISBN 0 946651 01 9

CONTENTS

Walk No.   **Page**

—   Dartmoor—Foreward and Onward!   5

1   From Meldon Reservoir where There's No Business Like Snow Business   7

2   A Dart Around the Teign   12

3   A Pilgrimage to the Foreign Lands of South Western Dartmoor (and the Royal Oak at Meavy)   16

4   To Dartmoor's North Pole—Fur Tor in February   19

5   The Tom Cobley Walk   24

6   The West/East Crossing (Dartmoor Inn, Lydford to Steps Bridge)   30

7   The Lich Way—The Way of the Dead . . . and the Dying!   37

8   The North/South Walk—Reversed...   42

9   Haytor Circular   50

10   Best of the Summer Wine—a Vintage Evening Walk from South Brent   59

11   From Whiteworks to Walkhampton and Back, Purely for Research   60

12   The Belstone Renard   68

13   A Walkham Walkabout   72

Tess.

14 Haytor—'Hippyocracy' and a Dartmoor Salvation ... 75

15 A Safari in the Dartmoor Desert 79

16 To Ducks' Pool via Heaven! 83

17 The Abbot's Way 88

18 New Habits—the Other Abbot's Way 95

19 New Boots, New Blisters and New Bridge 98

20 Throwleigh to Warren House in the Wet Monsoon
    Season 102

21 The Tavy Cleave and Rattlebrook—via Peking 106

—   Dartmoor Letterboxes—Signed, Sealed and
    Discovered 111

The Original Diaries— the source of these tales

Dartmoor—Foreward and Onward!

"To all of us there come days when the earth is stale, flat and tedious, when the net of life's petty restrictions strangles the spirit's last flutterings and when a crowd of fellow mortals affects one as a collection of hopeless and soulless oafs."
These feelings prompted Ray Cattell to take to the sea and write about his adventures experienced along the South Devon coastline. But as I am a non-swimmer, and therefore a committed landlubber, a similar philosophy has taken me inland to explore Dartmoor in all its moods and seasons.

Reflected in the many journeys into and around the Dartmoor heartland are tales to which many would-be Dartmoor explorers will relate. There are the inevitable fruits of fenland folly, the trials and tribulations of escorting ill-equipped foreigners on walks, and the delights and despairs of doing battle with Dartmoor's oft-times inclement weather. This is a personal diary of walks selected from a misspent youth of Dartmoor perambulation. Hopefully many readers will identify, and therefore sympathise, with the dilemmas which arise whilst it is hoped that everyone will enjoy this light-hearted appraisal of Dartmoor walking.

The format of the book is simple. Where possible, photographs, diagrams, drawings and 3-dimensional profiles account for much of the route description whereas the text examines the problems, pitfalls or pure joy at visiting these places. In particular the profiles provide a tremendous insight into the shape of Dartmoor's topography and could well prove a useful resource, when used in conjunction with OS maps, to enable walkers to plan their routes. Through these diagrams the moor is exaggerated to emphasise peaks, tors and valleys. Any walker who may be dumbfounded by the interpretation of contour lines will find salvation with these annotated sketches. Dartmoor has been labelled 'the unknowable' by many moorland experts. It is a modest hope that the detailed portfolio of illustrations will at least portray the many faces of Dartmoor.

The Tavy Cleave

1

From Meldon Reservoir where There's No Business Like Snow Business

It was one of those days when had we heeded the weathermen, we would not have ventured out of doors, leave alone visited Dartmoor. Meteorological soothsayers liberally placed snow symbols onto their charts and, using old and hackneyed euphemisms, proceeded to tell us that the early morning clear skies would soon give way to blizzard-like conditions on high ground. As 'Willy's' corns had not re-inforced this notion, and as my seaweed was non-committal, the group unanimously opted for an early start in the belief that we could scurry home quickly if needs be.

The sun was barely up at Meldon Reservoir but the scene was one of great beauty as we crossed the top of the dam in perfect walking conditions. A discussion arose about dams and their scenic contribution to the Dartmoor landscape, one which had so many emotive and statistical undertones that, at the end of the conversation on conservation below Homerton Hill, I could not say whether our forum was "for 'em" or "agin 'em".

To the north-east of Homerton Hill a small stream plunges exceedingly steeply into the reservoir. We used this as our short-cut to get to Black Tor. The initial upland struggle through this precipitous canyon is rewarded by an easy approach to the shelf-like Black Tor. Co-incidentally, on the opposite side of the West Okement is Shelstone Tor which literally means that.

Below Black Tor, on the rocky hillside, is Black Tor Copse, a small forest of stunted pendunculate oaks. The most famous of these unusual woods, on the moor, is Wistman's Wood, a mile north of Two Bridges, whilst a third stunted forest is to be found at Piles Copse in the Erme Valley. Although of great appeal to the botanist, they provide an obstacle for the walker because journeys through them are punctuated by slippery moss covered rocks, and branches which seem to reach out in an attempt to disfigure you.

From the impressive Black Tor we struggled manfully to Fordsland Ledge before finally scaling High Willhays, the highest point in the South of England, (apart from the top of the TV mast at Princetown, which we had no intention of scaling!).

J. Reynolds.

The morning was by now blossoming into one of the finest I had ever experienced on Dartmoor. The sunlit tors all looked only a step away. In the distance Exmoor had been dusted in a cover of snow which accentuated its outline. Apparently the Culm measures farm-land between the two moors had acted as a barrier, fending off the previous night's snow flakes.

The clarity of the view obviously impaired our judgement over which way we should travel. Cawsand Hill (or Cosdon), some 5 miles distant, appealed to us as a challenge to test our stamina. From this hill, once believed to be the highest on the moor, the views were even better than from High Willhays, which was more than reason enough for us to want to savour them.

We reached Steeperton with relative ease because we shamelessly followed the east-bound army track, a sort of 'Big dipper' across the moor. It was only the last few hundred yards up to the tor which caused us to consider the question "Was Dartmoor walking really worth the effort?" as the slope left us quite breathless.

On Steeperton there is an army hut which had a pile of coal and the facilities for lighting a fire. Inside it we were cosy, but cramped,

8

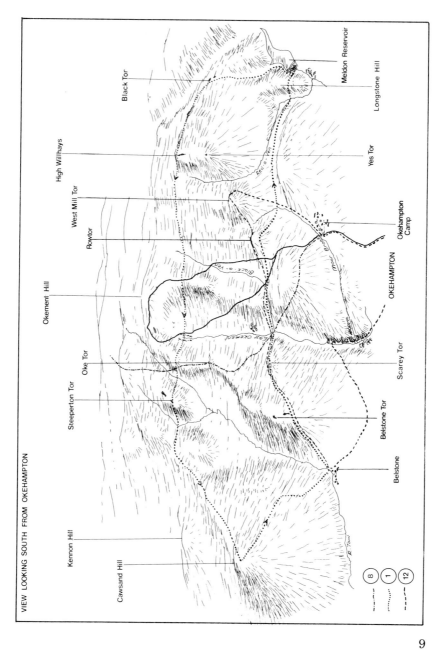

VIEW LOOKING SOUTH FROM OKEHAMPTON

9

whilst we had a warming cup of coffee and sang some traditional folk songs with untraditional lyrics.

Back outside again there was still Cawsand to be conquered so 'Fingers' quickly tossed the dregs from his cup into the wind, only to get them straight back again. Noting this incident, the others went behind a rock for personal reasons, but exhibited a little more care over the wind direction!

Hound Tor and its counterpart Little Hound Tor were passed by without incident. Although the climb up the magnificent Cawsand Hill is only a gentle one, from this direction, it still posed a tedious task with its long vegetation and awkward terrain. So intent were we on getting to the top that we miserably failed to notice a bank of cloud approaching from the north-east. Within a few moments of

A wintry view of Yes Tor and West Mill Tor

attaining the beacon the conditions dramatically changed. There was poor visibility and a swirling sleet converted the golden sunlight into a twilight darkness. Thoughts of Childe the Hunter, who perished inside the carcass of his horse during a blizzard, crossed my mind. Childe promised his estates to the persons who interred his body in consecrated ground, but I seriously doubted whether anyone would want my estates, a 10-year old Lambretta and an overdraft.

We quickly dropped from the summit of the hill and there was a brief respite as we got below the enveloping mist. Belstone was reached in record time as the sleet turned to large snowflakes, and the temperature had plummeted. We were worried because we knew we were a good step away from Meldon, so we adjourned to the Tors Hotel in Belstone to plan our strategy. The locals were discouraging as they shook their heads and said such things as, "Don't like the look of it—it's set in for days now", and "Glad we don't have to drive anywhere in this today". You could tell that we were subdued because we agreed to stop for a maximum of fifteen minutes and concentrated our indulgences on whiskies rather than pints—Dutch courage.

There were two schools of thought about our return route to Meldon. One cautious proposed route was along the road to Fatherford Viaduct and thence by path into Okehampton, from there the path across the golf course would have taken us to Meldon. However, two arguments were put forward against this proposal. Firstly, that to follow it would have meant a good deal of up and down walking to cover just under six miles, and secondly, a straighter proposed route across the moor necessitated a WSW walk which meant that the blizzard would simply blow into our backs, the least uncomfortable direction from which to endure a blizzard, and the thought of a wind assisted dash, of marginally under four miles, seemed infinitely preferable.

We left The Tors at one o'clock and with heads down, hoods up, and well clad, took on the full force of the elements with a latent sense of adventure. The beauty of Cullever Steps was not readily appreciated as we traversed the moor at a half running, half walking pace. We did not see any other tors or features as we contoured the lower northern slopes of Rowtor to reach Black Down. For once we were thankful for the army's tracks as one of them led us down to cross the Red-a-ven brook below Longstone Hill. Indeed the hardest part of this 45 minutes spurt was the effort needed to cross the spur of this hill.

There was no sign of life at Meldon Reservoir car park. We did not bother to take off our boots as we anticipated having to push our car at some point on the journey home. But fortunately the difficult journey was not impossible and we got back to Exeter after a celebratory cup of coffee at Bay Tree near Crockernwell—followed by a snowball fight.

For several days Okehampton and surrounding villages were cut off, and some ladies, who were nine months pregnant, were airlifted as part of an unusual 'delivery' service. The Dartmoor Rescue

Group were called out many times and on one occasion a clairvoyant was called upon to find a lost group. We learnt a lot from this near disaster and are now much wiser for the experience.

2

A Dart Around the Teign

It had been a bad winter for walking and life's little games had kept me busy with petty distractions. The weather, in past weeks, had played some wicked tricks whenever a walk was contemplated, hurling a barrage of meteorological nasties to keep us from walking on the moor.

Thus, with a feeling of deep desire to escape from the monotonous routine of everyday life, it was to Clifford Bridge in the Teign Valley that we repaired to get some therapeutic fresh air and exercise. The higher moors had been bombarded by blizzards and there was every chance another might sweep in from the turbulent Atlantic at any moment.

With that ominous beginning our first move was to visit a hidden valley called Halls Cleave, a valley that probably only a handful of walkers know exists. A small tributary of the Teign flows through this beautiful gorge to join the main stream at Clifford Bridge. Because the valley is private we asked permission to take the path through it and this was duly granted. The first quarter mile is somewhat claustrophobic as the steep sides and the dense canopy of trees unite to create an oppressive environment, but soon after turning due west the valley opens up.

There were four of us on this exploration and, as none of the others had been through Halls Cleave, they congratulated the navigator on his choice of route, as the temperatures were benevolently mild compared to the tundra conditions being experienced on the high moors only a dozen miles away to the west.

We followed the main track and climbed steeply upwards through the western side of Coleridge Wood. Beyond the thin cover of trees, on our right, were the farms of Wooston and Little Wooston. I knew them well as I had written my thesis about Mid Devon farms and, although not a rivetting subject, it had given me an excuse to study the countryside I knew and loved.

Still in the shelter of the forest, just before we exited onto the high, wind-swept Mardon Down, we had some hot coffee, laced with whisky. Walking manuals tell you to avoid alcohol as it lowers resistance. It certainly lowered mine because I had another cup and felt even more festive than usual! Although the temperatures were barely above freezing we were well insulated by thermal vests, track suit bottoms beneath our trousers, scarves, balaclavas, mittens and a stunning array of woollen garments. 'Willy' even has some of his mother's chutney, a proven remedy to repel any extremes of weather.

The intention of the morning session was to cover the high peaks, gently rounded hills, on the south side of the Teign Gorge. From Mardon Down, its higher western ridge, we descended to Coombe Court. Combe in a place name invariably means 'in a valley' and in this instance it was aptly named.

Our initial target was Butterdon Hill. We could have reached it by following a straighter line across the fields of Northmoor but years earlier I had 'got stugged' at the head of a small stream which rises there. (This quaint term applies to someone who has succumbed to being well and truly stuck in a bog.) Since then I have always avoided uncharted farmland.

At Butterdon the clouds had risen high enough to give a beautiful view to the stark bleak far-off northern moors. Hangingstone, Wild Tor, Watern Tor and other rocky friends could be identified in the grey distance. Some of the others wanted to visit nearby Willingstone Rock but time being short commonsense prevailed and we were soon at Cranbrook Castle. Such a grandiose name deserves a better fort, for this is little more than an elevated, glorified, mound surrounded by a ditch.

Beneath us to the south-west Chagford appeared as a cosy village nestled into some lovely hills and downs, notably Meldon Hill and Nattadon Common. Smoke drifted from the clustered houses as the snow-capped hills rose into an arctic crescendo beyond. We quickened our pace over Uppacott Down where the ruts of motorbike tyres could be clearly identified. No detection was necessary as one motorcross vandal swooped dangerously past us.

To descend the edge of Whiddon Woods, on the side of Whiddon

River Teign below Hunter's Tor

Park, is to stumble steeply downwards over the shoulder of a great and steep hill. I don't think we trespassed as we stuck to what we thought was semi-moorland. Our agility was tested by a few great walls before we finally reached the Teign below Hunter's Tor. The promise of alcoholic refreshment prompted a quick burst, along the fields beside the Teign, to Dogmarsh Bridge. To see grown men race to get to the Sandy Park Inn, with such cheerful determination, was certainly impressive. Less impressive however were our efforts, after a good few pints of ale, to play darts. The inn has a low ceiling that received a comprehensive bombardment whenever we aimed for doubles at the top of the board. On a number of occasions 'arrows' crashed spectacularly to the floor, missing the dartboard, the rubber tyre surround, and even the wall itself.

Thoroughly bamboozled, we trooped back along the fields beside the Teign towards Fingle Bridge. At Coombe we deviated from the river banks to mount the Hunter's Path, a gently climbing track up to Sharp Tor, which is a steep and precipitous outcrop. Castle Drogo perched on Piddledown Common certainly looked austere against the sky line but anyone who has visited it would appreciate its finer points. Lutyens certainly knew how to create a perfect Englishman's Home.

The magnificent Teign gorge was fully appreciated as we passed Hunting Gate to descend to a deserted Fingle Bridge. The talk was first of salmon and trout but then turned to wooden salmon and wooden trout. Many years ago Harry Price, who lived at Fingle Bridge, carved some fine specimens, facsimiles of original fish he had taken from the Teign. He believed that to stuff a fish was wasteful so consequently the walls of the Angler's Rest public

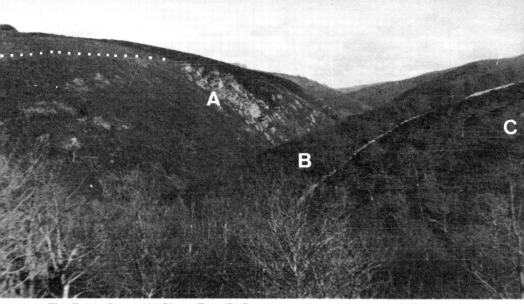

The Teign Gorge (A) Sharp Tor; (B) Dartington Trust Woodlands; (C) Edge of Whiddon Park. White dotted line is Hunter's Path

Looking westwards from Sharp Tor

house are adorned with wooden fish. Harry, who died in 1965, kept a diary of a Royal Tour (1901) he went on when he served with the Royal Navy on HMS Ophir. His artistic skills were also used to illustrate his observations on the voyage. His original diary has been published, resulting in a beautiful book.

The light was now fading as large snowflakes filled the air. As we were worried about the journey home we omitted a visit to Wooston Castle, another of the many Teign valley hill forts, in order to hurry back to our car at Clifford Bridge. The estimated 10.54 miles we had covered were splendid. Even though Dartmoor proper had been put 'out of bounds' by the elements, this lovely valley had provided adequate compensation. When we arrived home there were many reports about the blizzards which had closed roads on the western side of the moor. But the Teign Valley had seen very little sign of this wild weather.

— 3 —

A Pilgrimage to the Foreign Lands of South Western Dartmoor (and the Royal Oak at Meavy)

From time to time a wanderlust feeling stirs in my bones and causes me to venture into that foreign kingdom of the southwestern horizons of Dartmoor, a land of rolling hills fringed by a motley mixture of spoil heaps in the China Clay quasi-lunar landscape of Lee Moor.

Such a feeling comes about twice a year, just enough to kindle an affection for the distant quiet hills on that corner of the moor.

Having driven through Cornwood, en route, we found ourselves, by hook or by crook, at Rook. This weak, whimsical rhyme was particularly appropriate as in the lanes leading to this moorland location, just south of Penn Beacon, we were obliged to perform all manner of vehicular manoeuvres. The intricate network of lanes and tracks made navigating extremely difficult. 'Fingers', our driver, and 'Willy', our navigator gave each other a tough time before we finally settled for a mutually agreed car parking spot below Rook Tor.

From our lofty vantage point our immediate view was across to

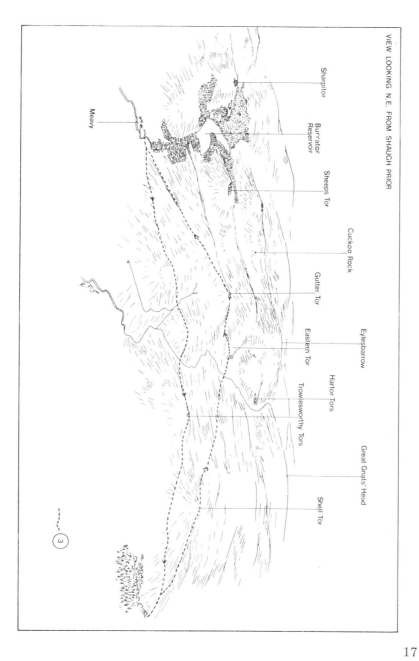

VIEW LOOKING N.E. FROM SHAUGH PRIOR

Sharpitor

Meavy

Burrator
Reservoir

Sheeps Tor

Cuckoo Rock

Gutter Tor

Eylesbarrow

Eastern Tor

Hartor Tors

Trowlesworthy Tors

Great Gnats' Head

Shell Tor

3

17

the amphitheatre shaped valley that yields south Devon a beautiful river, the Yealm. It was a good job that this early February morning was a cold, dry and sunny one for the climb up to Penn Beacon is long and steep. It provided a useful slope to warm and wake us up as it was barely light: the ensemble had all risen at 6.00 am in order to do a brisk stroll, and we were all still half asleep.

From Shell Top the ever-brightening scene gave majestic views towards Princetown and Tavistock. The unusual triangular pile of Hen Tor was visited and, after what seemed an eternity of searching, Mike found the letterbox and added some pertinent comments about the 'joys' of having to get up at such an unearthly hour, on a Sunday morning, especially following a late night out at a discotheque. However, a murmer of "The Royal Oak, Meavy" went around and a sudden transformation took place. Within seconds there was a spring in our steps—a troupe of born again walkers.

When we got to the Plym it had to be crossed, rivers always have to be. I can't use stepping stones, they always tip me off into the deepest pools, so I have a technique which uses the shallowest crossing. I simply wade across. A bootful or two of water of my own choice is infinitely preferable.

Beyond Eastern Tor the track which closely skirts Gutter Mire was followed. The topic of conversation was the time long ago when my friend 'Willy' led us into this mire and our good and absent friend, Clive, became well and truly 'stugged'. I had noticed Clive's predicament and in the dash to extricate him from a potentially watery grave only succeeded in being thrown backwards into the same mire. Whilst all these fun and games were taking place 'Willy' stood transfixed to the spot mesmerised by the scene. Slowly it dawned on him that we were not enjoying ourselves and he used his walking stick to good purpose to rescue us. A short while later we were grateful to the Royal Navy for allowing us to dry out by a lovely warm fire at their Ditsworthy Warren House. By the time this tale, and 'Willy's' version—an entirely different appraisal, had been recounted, we had traversed Ringmore Down and made our way down to the Royal Oak at Meavy.

From Meavy, a few hours and several pints later, we light-headedly climbed up to Lynch Common and made our way cheerfully to Legis Tor. Had it been summer we would have stopped for a sleep at Legis Tor or had a swim in the Plym but neither option

18

appealed to us on such a cold winter's day as this.

Trowlesworthy Tors, which resembles the rockpiles of Bodmin Moor, were fully explored. Anybody who cares to inspect the map and notices how we unashamedly followed the thousand foot contour almost back to Rook Tor will either praise us on our ability to contour quite a long distance, or criticise us for such an apparently dull route. In our defence it compensated for an early start by giving us an easy last few miles.

4

To Dartmoor's North Pole—Fur Tor in February

The snows of January were, by contrast, a mild interlude in this winter of cool discontent. February arrived with a wedge of high pressure which stubbornly refused to allow any warm air to waft over Britain. The old cliché "too cold for snow" was uppermost on our frozen lips as we travelled beneath clear blue skies to Two Bridges. The only snow to be found lay beneath walls facing northwards away from the weak winter sun.

The initial conversation was zoologically orientated with brass monkeys the main topic. Dartmoor was as cold as a deep freeze with all its bogs frozen solid. Those in sunlight had a crisp crunchiness about them although the heavier members of our entourage exhibited a certain wariness at the chances of a safe, dry passage across them.

There were no fellow countrymen about as we scrunched and slithered our way along the track northwards from Two Bridges. As we had no wish to visit the icy, frozen, bog kingdom, beside the West Dart, which leads up to Wistman's Wood, we gently ascended the side of the hill to Littaford Tors.

It was too cold to linger as we mounted Longford Tors, but the views across the sunlit moors were well worth the suffering. In normal circumstances outer garments are usually shed after a warming-up first mile, but today it was so cold that all spare items were utilised to good purpose. Mike even sported a long spare pair

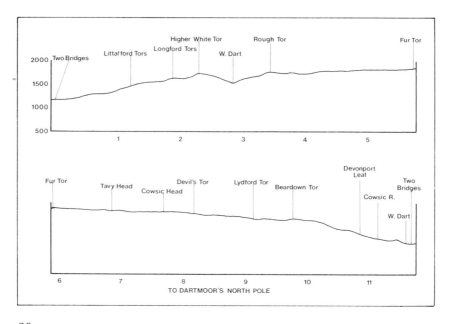

of woolly socks which went from his hands to his shoulders. I wore a spare sock on top of my balaclava and resembled a cross between a train robber and Wee Willy Winky. At least *we* knew where we wandered.

At Higher White Tor a debate ensued as to whether we crossed the tundra-like peat land fen to Dartmoor's equivalent of the North Pole, that is Fur Tor, or struggle westwards to 'rough it' at the inn at Merrivale. Strangely, for us, Fur Tor was selected for a number of reasons. Firstly, to pay good money for beer on a day when it would simply pass right through seemed a wanton waste, and secondly as we possessed hip flasks full of brandy and whisky, purely for medicinal purposes, we felt that Fur Tor had much to compensate it.

Besides, we were all keen to see the effect that the sub-zero temperatures would have on the giant peat hags around Tavy Head. We were not disappointed because the normally oozy mix between the hags was frozen so hard that we passed along the gullies instead of hopping across the tops of them—a strange, unnatural experience.

The going was still tough but the temperature, which had rocketed up to about minus three degrees centigrade, was more bearable than might be expected because of the dryness of the air.

To be able to describe the unbelievable dullness of the terrain to Fur Tor in a way which would make it exciting, or even seem inviting, is beyond my scope. Suffice it to say that the cross-section reveals the plateau-like nature of the terrain which would only be truly appreciated by the real Dartmoor enthusiast. It is a vintage wilderness today devoid of almost everything except frozen peat.

From Fur Tor's worthy mass of rocks, views extend towards the Tavy Cleave and northwards to the elevated peaks of northernmost Dartmoor. It is an oasis in the bleak tundra of this part of the moor. Six miles of hard walking was rewarded by a scene of unparalled beauty and a twenty minute break to consume a diet of hot soup, hot laced coffee, cheese sandwiches and lots of chocolate. Whilst we were there several people arrived from other parts of the moor to sign the visitors' book. The most popular origins seemed to be from Fernworthy or the Dartmoor Inn at Bridestowe. Everybody at Fur Tor seemed to agree that we had taken the least scenic route to this, the remotest tor on Dartmoor.

To get back to Two Bridges we traversed this much maligned cryogenic morass slightly west of the line that took us to Fur Tor. In practical terms the topography was a little more varied as both Tavy and Cowsic Heads provided a few extra dips in the terrain. Once the edge of the venn country is attained the whole landscape is transformed into steep valleys with impressive tors. As we had already sampled the delights of the Longford Tors ridge we decided to visit Devil's Tor, Lydford Tor (near the Lich Way) and the tremendous Beardown Tors. From the latter we descended through the convenient corridor in the plantation on the side of Beardown Hill to reach Bear Down Farm. Many puns were made but they do not bear mentioning here.

The romantic sounding Cowsic River curves around the southern spur of Beardown Hill to enter the West Dart at Two Bridges. Below the farm the valley is truly gorgeous, a place of extreme beauty. The Reverend Bray also appreciated this harmony with nature and dedicated certain rocks in and near the river to his favourite poets. Thus carved on many boulders in and near the River Cowsic are their engraved names, many though disappearing as the rocks are being eroded or weathered by the various elements. In a similar weather-beaten state we completed the last few hundred yards of the walk back to Two Bridges which had taken on the role of deep freeze owing to its shady location.

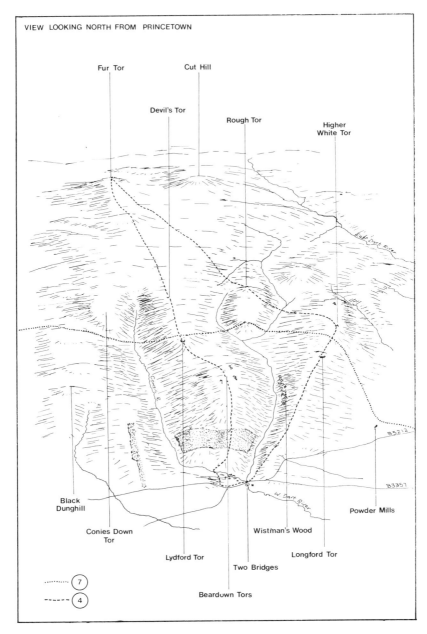

VIEW LOOKING NORTH FROM PRINCETOWN

Fur Tor   Cut Hill

Devil's Tor

Rough Tor

Higher
White Tor

East Dart River

Cowsic R.

B3212

B3357

Black
Dunghill

W Dart River

Powder Mills

Conies Down
Tor

Wistman's Wood

Lydford Tor

Longford Tor

Two Bridges

Beardown Tors

7

4

The Tom Cobley Walk

"Tom Pearce, Tom Pearce, lend me your grey mare?"

"No!" came the reply, so it was Shanks's Pony for us between the hilltop village of Spreyton, three miles outside of the National Park boundary, and Widecombe-in-the-Moor some twenty miles away. The assembled group were just as motley a crew as Tom Cobley's. In Spreyton there are plenty of names adopted from this local legend, moreso than in Widecombe. The pub is called The Tom Cobley and several cottages are named in a similar vogue.

As Widecombe Fair always takes place on the second Tuesday of September, and as our walks always set forth on a Sunday, a true journey could not be set up—nor of course could we follow a true route as we did not know it. Suffice it to say that we merely followed what we felt was a reasonably direct route of tracks, roads and some open moorland between the two points, all of which would amount to about 19 to 20 miles.

Whenever we do long strolls we select dates as close to the equinoxes as possible, for in spring or autumn there is about thirteen hours of daylight available. This is useful for getting lost and then found again and the likelihood of a blizzard or heatwave is minimised.

We passed the Church and those of us 30-strong group who were religiously inclined offered a prayer, whilst our more secular members cursed the early start, the dusty track, and anything else which sprang to mind.

Towards Nethercott, on a public right of way, fine views of the mighty Cawsand Hill were being snapped by our photographic enthusiasts. The derelict state of Nethercott Farm went unnoticed as we made good time southwards on a track of varying ups and downs, twists and turns, which was sufficiently interesting to make the proceedings worthwhile.

The map suggested a direct route through Coursebeer but as our scout had experienced difficulty in these parts, a few weeks previous, we felt it more diplomatic to skirt it following the two long sides of a triangle. Thoroughly conversant with Pythageras we realised that the extra sprint to Brandis Cross had prolonged the stroll.

The track to Addiscott was taken even though it ran east/west and we were keen to go north/south. However, we were soon back on course. We crossed the A30 at Fire Stone Cross and made excellent time along the quiet lane to East Week.

Beyond East Week we descended the small, but wonderfully sheltered, valley of the Blackaton Brook. That is, it is sheltered when the westerlies prevail and today the temperatures in the Throwleigh area were most noticeably higher than earlier at windswept Spreyton. As one of the troop was always 'game for a laugh' we had labelled her the 'old grey mare'. At least she fulfilled two-thirds of the description but we will not reveal which two. Anyhow, every time we sang the folk song she sportingly got down on all fours. But in Throwleigh when we burst into song she baulked at performing in full view of the locals, and the 'old grey mare' got three faults for a refusal.

An excrutiatingly muddy lane took us to Wonson and a well earned drink at the lovely North Moor Arms. The map reader and leader (me) was congratulated for managing to arrive at this spot at the precise moment of opening time. Fifteen minutes and a 'quick quart' later the much merrier band staggered past the sober sounding Providence Place and turned right to drop sharply down in a deep combe and thence steeply up to the youth-hostel at Gidleigh. One misguided, beer-influenced fellow had actually thought that the red triangle, representing the YHA building on the map, was in fact a sign for a Bass pub. The unfortunate fellow was dragged beyond this and onto the lovely woodland path which curves beneath Gidleigh Tor and across the Teign. Most of the way we had taken was the Mariners Way but as we did not wish to taunt our alcoholic friend we abstained from singing renditions of "Yo ho ho and . . ."

Dennis Johnston, our scout, had walked, and re-walked, several sections of this stroll and had also sampled various alternatives for us to have a smooth journey. From Teigncombe he had tried routes via Kes Tor and Thornworthy as well as the track above Ford Park to Frenchbeer. After consultation we took what we believed to be the 'lazybones route' along the apparently easy-to-follow track to Frenchbeer. Alas, some 'x-rated' horror bogs soon made us regret the soft option. The 1:25000 map labels the place as Boldventure, which is about right. In true British spirit we squelched on uncomplainingly to emerge at Frenchbeer triumphant but stugged in unidentifiable substances of the miry kind. I had worried about crossing the South Teign as my success rate with stepping stones is non-existent. Fortunately, a strategically located footbridge enabled me to avoid the embarrassment of falling in.

Beyond Yardworthy we reached the road from Chagford to Fernworthy. The Mariners Way continues below open moorland on tracks past places like Hurston and Jurston. The two names if

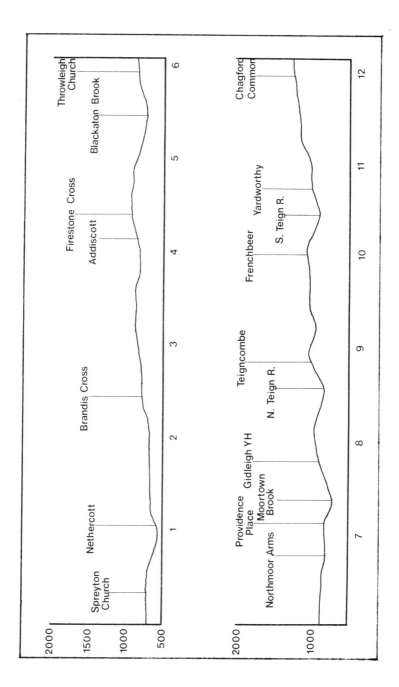

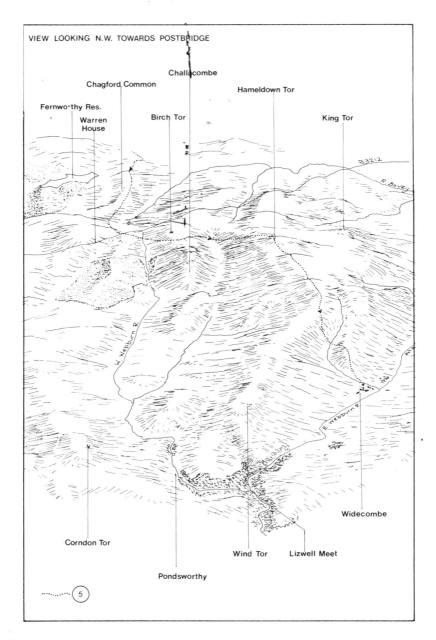

VIEW LOOKING N.W. TOWARDS POSTBRIDGE

Challacombe

Chagford Common

Hameldown Tor

Fernworthy Res.

Warren House

Birch Tor

King Tor

B3212

R Bovey

W Webburn R.

E. Webburn R.

Widecombe

Corndon Tor

Wind Tor

Lizwell Meet

Pondsworthy

5

pronounced by a Spaniard or Mexican might cause some confusion—perhaps that's why they are so close together. But here we left the well-worn track for pastures new.

Semi-claustrophobic walking tendencies prevailed as the pilgrims opted for open moorland in preference to tracks for the remainder of the 'ride' to Widecombe. The deviation across Chagford Common immediately resulted in a hard slog. The rising terrain drained the energy so much that at the Warren House several fatigued ramblers dropped out and stayed on the coach. The next few miles were a pleasant contrast as we took the path across the old tin mine workings to Headland Warren. At Grimspound we sat in the remains, the Bovis of the Bronze Age Dartmoor settlements and gathered breath for the assault on Hameldown, the last climb of the day.

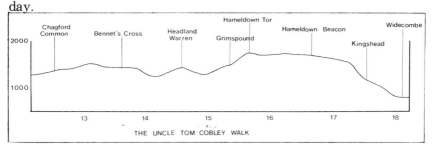

THE UNCLE TOM COBLEY WALK

The great lump of Hameldown, recognisable from afar, is a friend to walkers as once its summit is surmounted it gives an easy walk along its ridge with superb views all around. The terrain is such that you can actually lift up your eyes and survey the wondrous scene.

We left Hameldown via a path past Kingshead which drops

steeply down to Widecombe. Even though it was early in the tourist season there were still many visitors helping to make Widecombe look busy. It was unlikely that any of them would have guessed the nature of our walk, or even have known about the precise journey supposedly taken by Tom Cobley and friends to get to Widecombe.

Widecombe

Unlike the famous folk heroes, who rode so recklessly into Widecombe, we could not enjoy excessive alcoholic refreshment at the end of *our* journey as both of the pubs were closed, so we went soberly home.

6

The West-East Crossing (Dartmoor Inn, Lydford to Steps Bridge)

Why, you may enquire, is this a west/east crossing and not an east/west crossing? Well, it is because as a geographer and an exponent of meteorological and climatic principles, I am conversant with the fact that in South-west England the prevailing wind is that of the westerly type. This, of course, would theoretically give us a helping hand. However, when we 'dropped anchor' at the Dartmoor Inn you can imagine our horror to find ourselves facing a force nine easterly gale. When 'Willy', my soul compatriot, and I emerged from the sheltered land near the Dartmoor Inn onto the down above

Widgery Cross, Brat Tor

the River Lyd it was as much as we could do to put one foot in front of the other. With about twenty miles to go it was a daunting prospect to be blown backwards one step for every two steps forward.

Brat Tor's extremely steep slopes, the sort you could crawl up on hands and knees during heatwaves, provided some shelter but when we popped our heads up above the line of Widgery Cross the gale promptly plucked off 'Willy's' hat and playfully carried it back to the bottom of the hill. He made a token gesture of retrieving it but had to capitulate to the March gales.

How we got to Great Links is a mystery as our garments ballooned into massive proportions making us appear like Michelin men battling across the moor. My own theory on our success at reaching Great Links was attributed to the fact that this was my favourite tor and enticingly offered sufficient shelter to take refreshment in relative comfort. The view across the whole of Bodmin Moor was fantastic revealing the prominent landmarks of Brown Willy, Rough Tor and Brown Gelly. My only regret was that it was too dangerous to climb to the summit of the tor as we would surely have been blown off. Even the trig point was unattainable such was the force of the wind.

We passed Dunnagoats and wondered about the origin of their names. 'Willy', a person who enjoys a pun or two, said "I dunna know" in a pseudo-Italian fashion. Walking manuals insist that in difficult conditions it is important to keep up morale so with wit like that we almost gave up there and then. At Bleak House we met another walker who kindly took a photograph of us. He was wisely walking westwards and was being literally blown along.

We skirted Green Tor and followed the curve of Amicombe Hill (or Knoll) before straightening our course towards Great Kneeset. Within minutes our walking speed was slowed even further by the nature of the countryside which confronted us. An extensive area of

Bleak House

blanket bog, or venn country, covers a great proportion of the northern moor. To cross it demands a new concept in walking. The technique is called 'bog hopping' which suggests energetic frolics into the air with the expectancy of lightly landing on terra firma. Reality however is less simplistic as usually the hummocks you land on rapidly subside into the morass with only the slightest provocation.

We deliberately veered to the left (or north) of Cranmere Pool so that we could easily locate it by tracking along the clear grassy corridor of the West Okement which starts almost at the pool. I signed the book 'James Perrot' and dated it 1854 to see if there would by any response to such a celebrated Cranmere signature. The visitors' books for Cranmere Pool are housed at Plymouth Library when full and 'Willy' had actually been there to examine them and enjoyed a quiet titter or two at the various witticisms which filled the pages of past volumes. His own father had been instrumental in rebuilding the box at Cranmere many years ago thus forging a genuine attachment with this highly vaunted venue.

Cranmere Pool

The sodden nature of the ground up to Hangingstone Hill soon made us lose that feeling of nostalgia. Had there been time we would have ambled over to the strangely bedded Watern Tor but as we had planned for a little light refreshment at Chagford the route became direct and the pace quickened. The crossing of the North Teign River below Hew Down was a fiasco as, frustrated by the lack of non-slip stepping

32

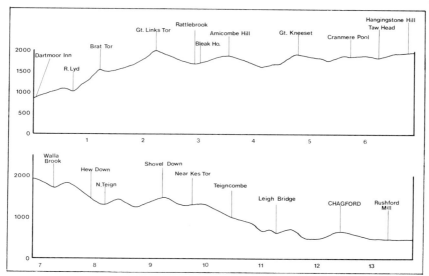

stones, I waded across the icy river. Kes Tor was passed by on our right hand side as we dropped sharply to Teigncombe. Not possessing spectacles the signs along the paths seemed to say "Trespassers will be congratulated" so we continued along a track to Leigh Bridge.

Road walking took us past Holystreet Manor and on into Chagford, ancient stannary town, floral village and former potato capital of Dartmoor. In the howling wind and driving rain of this grim March day it also appeared a ghost town. We rendezvoued with my wife who, having conveniently passed her driving test the day before, was acting as chauffeur and was also bravely crossing the width of the moor on her first solo driving expedition. We adjourned briefly to the Ring O' Bells for the swiftest of drinks and as the wind abated and the rain eased, we felt relatively comfortable walking out of Chaggyford—as one local had been heard to call it.

There were no frills to the afternoon session's walking—if a puddle was there, so be it, splash or drown, so intent were we to get to Steps Bridge with the minimum of ceremony. The beauty of the Teign Gorge would be there for us to savour another time. We reached the Teign at Rushford Farm and used the path through the fields to Dogmarsh Bridge at Sandy Park. The gorge presented itself half a mile ahead of us.

Chagford

Near Whiddon Park we crossed the Teign and followed the track on the south side of the river. Distance-wise it is slightly further than the elevated Hunter's Path but the thought of any unnecessary uphill going, after the day's proceedings, was out of the question. In our minds the Teign dropped down to Steps Bridge and that psychologically boded well for us. Not a soul had ventured to Fingle Bridge and the public toilets were closed, fortunately the bushes were not.

In about 45 minutes we were at Clifford Bridge. Its name fails to conjure up an image of the great surroundings which sets it off. 'Willy', always good for a quaint turn of phrase and a past master at the art of 'stating the bleeding obvious', said of Clifford Bridge as we approached it, "We'll cross that bridge when we come to it." Having fulfilled his prophecy we took the road towards Dunsford, maintaining a close liaison with the Teign on the riverside path through Dunsford Woods. Through this shadowy twilight world we galloped over gnarled tree trunks in rejuvenated style. At Steps Bridge we emerged on the eastern side of the Dartmoor National Park having now crossed it in both directions.

Even though the walk was done in oft-times atrocious conditions it was worth witnessing the immense variety of landscape within the Dartmoor National Park.

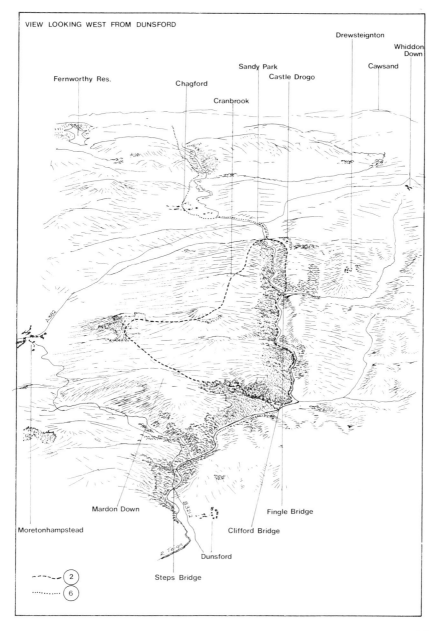

VIEW LOOKING WEST FROM DUNSFORD

Drewsteignton

Whiddon Down

Fernworthy Res.

Sandy Park

Castle Drogo

Cawsand

Chagford

Cranbrook

Mardon Down

Fingle Bridge

Moretonhampstead

Clifford Bridge

Dunsford

Steps Bridge

2

6

Fingle Bridge

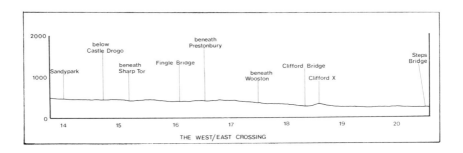

Sandypark

below
Castle Drogo

beneath
Sharp Tor

Fingle Bridge

beneath
Prestonbury

beneath
Wooston

Clifford Bridge

Clifford X

Steps
Bridge

THE WEST/EAST CROSSING

7

The Lich Way—The Way of the Dead . . . and the Dying!

My Dartmoor walking colleagues are as merry a bunch of persons as ever you are likely to meet and when I proposed that we should follow a variation of the route known as the Lich Way they thought it a marvellous idea and not the least bit macabre. For the un-initiated Lydford was and is the largest of Dartmoor parishes occupying an immense portion of Northern Dartmoor's wilderness. The once important settlement of Lydford is tucked snugly away into the western shoulder of the moor away from the rigours and full force of frequent tempestuous moorland weather. As it was deemed necessary to bury the dead in Lydford parish churchyard it created a situation where a reverential journey across this huge parish took on distance proportions unparalleled in other areas. The special dispensation, given to residents in ancient tenements like Babeny, of being able to arrange burials at Widecombe, meant that funeral processions from the south-eastern corner of the parish were rare.

To savour the atmosphere of this journey we arrived at Bellever, a

37

mile south of Postbridge, to pick up the funeral path at a spot where it probably crossed the East Dart.

In decidedly man-made coniferous surroundings we began our sombre journey. The first mile or so was improvised through the woods in a westerly direction which brought us out on the B3212 at the Cherry Brook.

With not a single 'Hairy Hand' in sight we followed a line close to the banks of the stream towards the Powder Mills. Any deviation may have created an early watery grave as the terrain was like a giant sponge of the non-edible kind.

Powder Mills

One of our crew told the story of Silas Sleep who was employed at the Powder Mills in the middle of the nineteenth century. The manufacture of gun powder was such a precarious occupation that there was every chance that a day's work might be rudely interrupted by an explosion. Silas Sleep, being a prudent perceptive person, who abhorred waste of any kind, would thus devour his breakfast, lunch and tea first thing in the morning lest he should become an unwilling customer for the Lich Way. Whether or not the saga is true I do not know, but it is thought that workers arriving at the entrance to the Powder Mills had to remove boots with metal bottoms so as not to cause any sparks.

In a short time we had left the Powder Mills way below us and reached the heights of Longford Tors. This part of the West Dart Valley is very beautiful. Many people visit this location to see the rare charm of Wistman's Wood, the subject of so much study, speculation and even suspicion. For me the view is all about the tors of strange shapes and profiles. This ridge is strewn with various peaks, some trivial and unchristened whilst the more notable have such names as Littaford Tors and Higher and Lower White Tors. The view is an orgy of tors and horizons for the Dartmoor connoisseur. We deviated to take in Crow Tor, perched on the hillside above us. The rough nature of the ground made us glad that we were not bearing a coffin.

On a less sombre note, the next few miles of somewhat dull walking were animated by a marathon session of puns related to the nature of the walk. Each and everyone of the company were guilty of contriving some of the most wicked remarks that could be imagined. It was all triggered off quite innocently when someone enquired "Which tor is closest to the dead centre of Dartmoor?" A post mortem followed to see who had exhumed the best witticism but nobody would undertake such a grave title. Some of the remarks

Crow Tor

departed from the spirit of things whilst others were real goners shrouded in mystery. It seemed an eternity before we passed on to happier hunting grounds and well and truly buried this moribund subject.

The track is not very well defined apart from odd short stretches. However, where it crosses the Walkham at a ford the path is at its widest and we utilised this as far as the White Barrow on Cocks Hill. The fierce westerly wind, which had done its best to impede our progress in the morning session, was given some time off as we sheltered behind a small burial mound. The more energetic and adventurous members of our group had engineered an alternative route via Peter Tavy or more precisely The Peter Tavy Inn, a fine hostelry with a celebrated range of traditional ales.

We bade them farewell and set off in a north-westerly direction towards Bagga Tor. The combination of a satisfying packed lunch and a good downhill spell united to produce a good pace. At

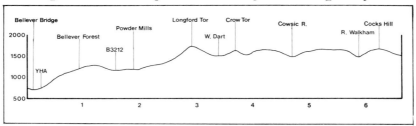

Browsentor Farm we left what was probably the original route that crossed the Tavy further upstream.

Hill Bridge is a rare beauty spot, one not invaded by the masses because there is little space to park a car. The mines and quarries of the nearby Mary Tavy area received their source of power from the leat which runs from the Tavy at this point. The Tavy is supposedly the second fastest flowing river in England and no doubt provided a good head of water. Today the same leat provides the driving force for a hydro-electric power plant, one of only three in Devon. Such little gems of knowledge were readily absorbed by those amongst us with an industrial archaeological bent.

All thermos flasks were empty by now and many eyed their emergency rations with intent. As it was beginning to rain quite heavily there seemed little to detain us so we followed the climbing, twisting track through some riding stables to Zoar. The gentle

Hill Bridge, River Tavy

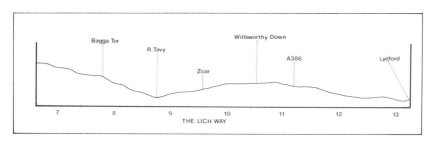

gradient back onto the open moor was easily negotiated as we emerged on featureless Kingsett Down near a most unusually shaped service reservoir.

Black Down and Willsworthy Camp is heavily scarred with tracks rendering the moor less wild and more unnatural than it should be. However, as we approached the A386 at Willsworthy Camp we were too tired to voice our protest at the obvious army despoilment of this area.

At Watervale we took the public right-of-way to Ingo Brake but were guilty of not examining the map sufficiently. Instead of

41

directly entering Lydford we discovered that the path veered away to the south-west along the old railway track. However, despite being called some unprintable names, I led the merry bunch into Lydford and threatened them with a further detour around Lydford Gorge. I think they almost believed me. Suffice it to say that appropriately enough they were all dead on their feet as they 'strode' into Lydford. Historians will appreciate this pun.

8

The North/South Walk—Reversed

Dartmoor has one square mile for each day of the year or, in simple terms, it occupies a large space just south-west of the centre of Devon. Its largest dimension is from north to south between Okehampton and Ivybridge, a distance of about thirty miles. There is a distinctly prestigious feel about being able to complete a journey between the two extremities of the moor in a day. The official North/South walk is something of a misnomer as it starts about six miles into the moor at Okement Hill. A more relevant statistic is that this organised stroll begins 1856 feet above sea level taking the initial sweat out of the early proceedings. The theory of doing it in a N/S direction is, psychologically, that it appears downhill. Being contrary beggars, my friends and I opted to do it S/N and here is the tale of that struggle which may, or probably may not, persuade others to follow in our footsteps.

If you work on these assumptions you will appreciate the strategy required for such a longer-than-marathon walk. (1) Thirty miles is a long way, (2) there are considerable gaps both in time and miles between pubs, (3) we do not walk very fast and (4) we like to enjoy the scenery.

At Bittaford we waved goodbye to our chauffeur who had picked us up in Exeter at 6.00 am and deposited us at the aforementioned spot some forty minutes later. As Bittaford is not exactly the Las Vegas of Dartmoor there is not much else to do at that time of day on a Sunday, so we thought that we might as well walk to Okehampton. Although we could have got out of the car some considerable

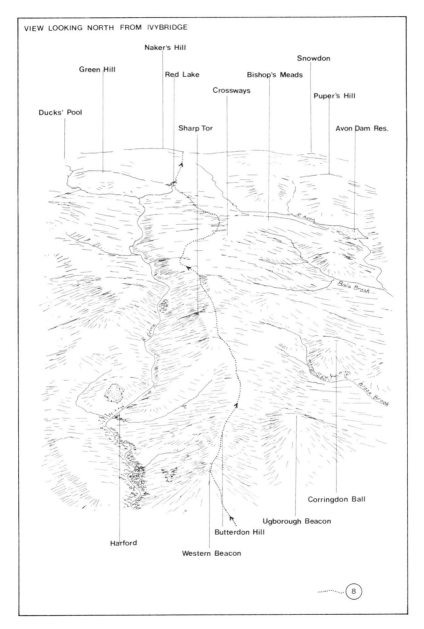

VIEW LOOKING NORTH FROM IVYBRIDGE

Naker's Hill

Green Hill

Red Lake

Snowdon

Bishop's Meads

Crossways

Puper's Hill

Ducks' Pool

Sharp Tor

Avon Dam Res.

R. Avon

Bala Brook

Brue Brook

Corringdon Ball

Ugborough Beacon

Butterdon Hill

Harford

Western Beacon

8

43

distance above the engineering works on the lane to Western Beacon we felt that the true crossing had to be from the old A38 road right across the moor to the old A30. This honest spirit of adventure rendered us breathless at the top of that lane.

At Western Beacon we paused to examine the early morning mists in the far off valleys of the South Hams. We thought about all those sleepyheads still in the land of nod (or commonsense) dreaming their dreams whilst we sat like lofty overlords, custodians of the southern part of England's most beautiful county. The other reason we sat was to have our breakfast as the early start had meant two of our five being pulled out of bed hurriedly, another being kicked out by his wife. As the daylight improved we could see that in his rush he had fastened his buttons to the wrong button holes and looked in sad disarray.

The topic of conversation centred around the annual race from Ivybridge up to Western Beacon and back down to Ivybridge again. Our group's opinions ranged from admiration, through to contempt and envy.

We made a ꜱee-line past the small non-Lancastrian spot known as Black Pool and on to Butterdon Hill. The going underfoot was excellent and continued to be so all the way to the Red Lake tramway. Several television film crews have used this tramway for access into the inner southern moor. On one occasion, 'Willy' a member of the team on this stroll, walked straight across a scene that John Earl was shooting and caused him to need another take. Mr Earl was somewhat peeved. The Red Lake tramway is 7½ miles long and contours the hills above the beautiful Erme Valley as far as the Red Lake clay pits. The undeniably great Dartmoor expert, Richard Hansford Worth, engineered the route which opened about 1910 and closed several times, the last occasion being in 1933 when the system was dismantled. For inexperienced walkers the track can be a blessing in thick fogs but for our part it served the function of getting us in good time across several miles of countryside and well on our way.

From Redlake more conventional walkers take the Fox Tor By-pass and enter the Northern Moor at Two Bridges either via Nun's Cross Farm or Royal Hill. Policeman Mike, who runs cross country daily, was all for legging it across the dreaded Foxtor Mire. 'Willy', the thinker, knew how to read maps and shared a distinct

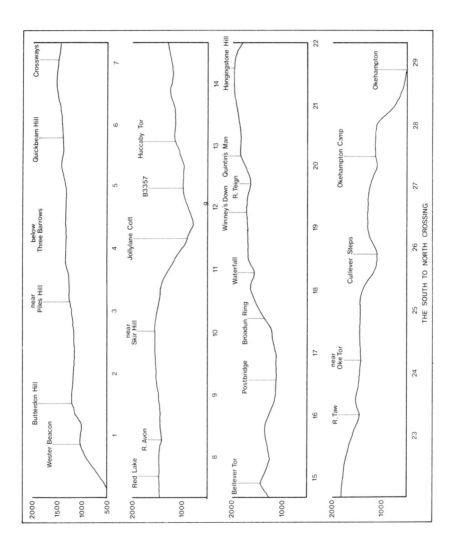

THE SOUTH TO NORTH CROSSING

Butterdon Hill · Wester Beacon · near Piles Hill · below Three Barrows · Quickbeam Hill · Crossways

Red Lake · R. Avon · near Skir Hill · Jollylane Cott · B3357 · Huccaby Tor

Bellever Tor · Postbridge · Broadun Ring · Waterfall · Winney's Down · R. Teign · Quintin's Man · Hangingstone Hill

R. Taw · near Oke Tor · Cullever Steps · Okehampton Camp · Okehampton

inclination for a lunch time session whilst 'Fingers', who couldn't run, or read maps, but possessed a compass, voted for a bearing to Hexworthy. And so it was that after much persuasive discussion we followed the Avon towards its miry head. Ter Hill and Skir Hill was bisected with ease. We ignored the invitation to descend into the valley of the O or Wo Brook although the terrain was exceedingly soft. But mention of its name led several members of the group to burst into song with "Oh wo wo" in them. There was a Helen Shapiro song followed by another oldie called "I don't want to go to the party tonight". This summed up the jocular spirit and morale of the group, so important for a trek of this length.

We descended Down Ridge and passed the Forest Inn, not yet open, still singing. The little cottage known as Jolly Lane Cott, the last Dartmoor building 'built in a day', was duly noted. This cottage was built on mid-Summer's day in 1835 by Tom and Sally Satterley, with a little help from their friends. It gave them the credentials needed to escape from their 'tied' employment. Fortune smiled on them as for several months they gathered and hid away the necessary building materials in various caches, ditches and other useful hidey-holes. These remained undetected until the day of the Holne Ram Roasting ceremony when the moorland farmers were otherwise distracted. By sunset the dwelling was complete with smoke being emitted from the chimney. This was a necessary formality and not a reflection on the Dartmoor climate of Victorian times. The Satterley family lived a happy life at Jolly Lane and the house is still in their hands. In tuneless disharmony 'Fingers' appropriately gave us a rendition of the cooker song "Home, home on the Range".

The 'grockle-trap' of Hexworthy was well patronised. Huccaby Tor was much quieter than Huccaby Bridge so we paused there to boost up our energy reserves with some food and drink. Although Bellever Tor is one of our favourite rockpiles we were aware that Postbridge was bestowed with certain refreshment facilities lacking at the tor. We were not tempted into the forest by the colour coded posts beckoning walkers onto intricately woven forest paths. Marching straight through the wide, dull but functional, fire break at regimental pace enabled us to reach Postbridge at a respectable hour.

The East Dart Hotel was our mecca and knowing of their

Huccaby Bridge, Hexworthy

somewhat tepid way of receiving Dartmoor walkers we hid our rucksacks, combed our hair, adjusted our clothes and mingled with the crowd in the bar. We had our quota of ale before we were twigged as walkers and wishing all a cheerful and sincere "Good day" bid farewell to our host, the bar steward, to retrieve our hidden rucksacks. At least we had worked up a genuine thirst, unlike most of the clientele!

I must confess that the first hour of afternoon walking was full of ribald tales and frequent dashes to inspect the flora and fauna behind stone walls. It is said that we followed the East Dart to Broadun Ring, scrambled up over Broad Down and then plunged into the waterfall (known as Marsh Falls) below Sandy Hole Pass. This sobering experience restored our memories and revived us for the sun had come out and, although it was only early May, we found it hot going.

All of us, except Mike, were extremely tired and a debate ensued as to what should be done and where. The old cliché of so near but so far seemed appropriate. After some talking the group opted for an arduous straight line to Hangingstone Hill. This 3½ miles across the side of Winneys Down, up the spur of Quentin's Man, and over Whitehorse Hill to the flag pole on Hangingstone took nearly two hours. The going was most difficult as the constantly damp terrain usurped our energy. As a consequence the conversation almost ran dry apart from short sharp sudden bursts of swearing, the good humoured variety. We knew we had to keep going and the peat pass over Whitehorse Hill provided a short respite before we adjourned for a well earned rest at Hangingstone.

According to the old Tourist Map of Dartmoor, 1983 is the Year of the Hangingstone Hill because of its height above sea-level when given in feet! Seriously though, this high point of our S/N crossing

Looking North from Postbridge (A) Broad Down; (B) Hartland Tor

was psychologically refreshing as we now had to descend from a little under 2000 feet to under 500 feet at Okehampton some seven miles distant. This down hill trend was also made easier by a good track to Oke Tor and beyond to Cullever Steps. By some miracle our morale soared and we got into a steady walking rhythm again of between two to three miles per hour. The late afternoon sun was weak in its power which aided our progress from a shadowy Cullever Steps to Okehampton Camp. By now the light was failing as villages in Mid-Devon could be identified by their lights. We took the artillery road down into Okehampton only deviating once onto a path down to the railway station.

We had done it. A portion of chips, a pint of shandy, and a hot foamy bath was followed by a sleep that would have done Rip Van Winkle proud.

48

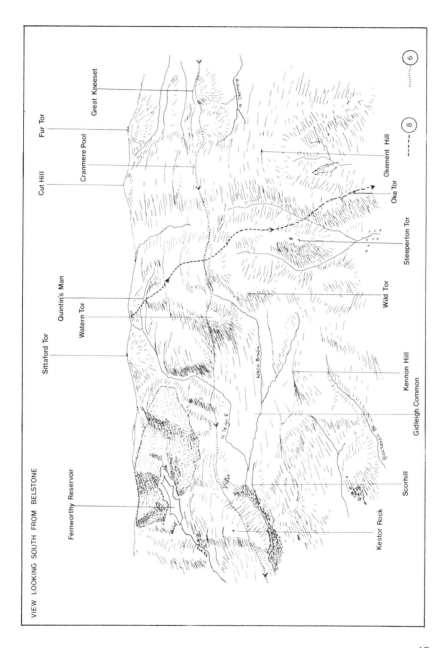

VIEW LOOKING SOUTH FROM BELSTONE

Fernworthy Reservoir

Sittaford Tor

Quintin's Man

Watern Tor

Cut Hill

Cranmere Pool

Fur Tor

Great Kneeset

Kestor Rock

Scorhill

Gidleigh Common

Kennon Hill

Wild Tor

Steeperton Tor

Oke Tor

Okement Hill

N Teign R

Walla Brook

Blackaton Br

N Okement

⑥ ⋯⋯⋯

⑧ ⸺⸺

49

9

Haytor Circular

After parking amidst the hordes at Haytor we immediately showed the quality of contrariness by turning our backs on the well-worn tracks and rocks of this beautiful down. It was to Bag Tor that we trundled, an easy and gentle descent to a small pile overlooking the valley of the River Sig. This river begins in an extremely boggy hollow just below Saddle Tor, a half mile to the west, and flows for all of two miles before joining the River Lemon. It has the distinction of being wooded for most of its course and has the tiny hamlet of Sigford named after it. This area beneath the moor is worth exploring when the upland conditions are extreme, for the borderland valleys always seem relatively mild.

Today though, the weather was kind and there was a distinct air of enthusiasm in our ranks which suggested that a longish stroll was in prospect. After picking our way across the steep hillside of the Sig Valley we hastened south-westwards along a track towards the disused rifle range, a mile to the south of Rippon Tor. Along this section the view is always impressive—the plateau of Little Haldon acts as a shoulder above the glinting waters of the Teign Estuary whilst beyond, tankers were spied in the Channel. As the eye follows the view around, the seven hills of Torquay give way to the familiar landmarks of Berry Head and Tor Bay. For those who know their Devon topography the castle at Totnes can be identified whilst the Day Mark on the National Trust land near Kingswear is also prominent. Even beyond this the South Hams falls away in gentle undulations. Unfortunately, as I enjoyed this panoramic scene I failed to notice a large boulder and ended up unceremoniously enjoying a faceful of Dartmoor granite, though with less enthusiasm.

On reaching the road we turned towards Cold East Cross but soon altered course again to cross Buckland Common and make the pilgrimage to Buckland Beacon. The word pilgrimage is used deliberately as the Ten Commandments are carved out of the rock.

A great local landowner and devout Christian, Mr Whitley employed Arthur Clement, in the summer of 1928, to carve the Ten

or as God said to Moses . . .

Keep taking the tablets!

Commandments on to two tablets at the Beacon. The idea was the result of the defeat in the Houses of Parliament of the Revised Prayer Book, the dates of the readings of this Bill are recorded for posterity. Alas, God's elements are dissolving the words on these weather-worn stones and their message is becoming difficult to decipher, and without renovation the marvellous efforts of Arthur Clement will disappear.

The next miles of walking are some of the easiest that Dartmoor can offer. We struck out northwards and soon reached the momentum of stride so essential in making light out of long walks. We transcended Pudsham Down and followed its semi-ridge elevation to the cairn at Blackslade Down. This particular route was chosen as years earlier we had spent an awful hour or so wallowing in

Bonehill Rocks and Honeybag Tor

Blackslade Mire. The OS map gives it one blue bog-like symbol which is a gross underestimation of the quaking nature of this foul pit. By contrast the upland route we followed was scenic and perfect for walking. Pil Tor and Top Tor are small piles but yield good views, especially down into the East Webburn Valley where Widecombe-in-the-Moor seemed to be in a winter hibernation from the masses of visitors who follow in the wake of Tom Cobley and his overcrowded mare.

The good walking terrain extends to Bonehill Down, a lovely atmospheric spot where the mountain range of Bell, Chinkwell and Honeybag Tors dominate the landscape. On this day these peaks were not for us as we crossed north-eastwards to Hound Tor, the most extensive pile of rocks on Dartmoor. Looking back to

52

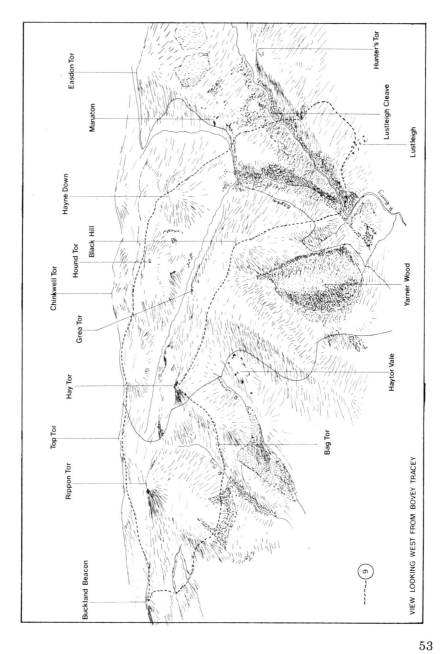

Easdon Tor

Manaton

Hunter's Tor

Lustleigh Cleave

Lustleigh

Hayne Down

Chinkwell Tor

Hound Tor

Black Hill

Grea Tor

Yarner Wood

Hay Tor

Haytor Vale

Top Tor

Rippon Tor

Bag Tor

Buckland Beacon

VIEW LOOKING WEST FROM BOVEY TRACEY

53

From Hayne Down towards Manaton

Honeybag we could see graceful hang gliders soaring and swooping on the thermals. Secretly I was envious of them but as I happen to be a devout coward, I took solace that my feet were much safer on the ground.

A short stretch of road walking gave us access to Hayne Down. Bowerman's Nose on its north-western corner is worth a visit but so is the Cleave Hotel at Lustleigh and thus we continued onwards over the down and anon to Water. Although the Kes Tor Inn is one of our regular haunts it was not, alas, opening time for we had made such good time that even a swift half or quick quart could not be countenanced. Beyond Water are the extensive woodlands of Lustleigh Cleave. Each section of wood has its own name and its own maze of tracks and paths, some officially signposted, others of pixie fashion which can lose and disorientate even the most well-intentioned perambulists. We knew our way and followed the wettest of all the paths—easily mistaken for a stream in winter—down to the River Bovey where a clam spans the stream. It is the main track through these woods and is the most direct to Lustleigh. The route

54

Looking up the Bovey Valley towards Lustleigh Cleave

is well signposted to the village so we did not have recourse to consult our cartographic oracle.

Lustleigh was entered by footpath, one of scores in the parish. The village is one of the most beautiful in Devon and makes Widecombe look plain by comparison with far more to please the discerning visitor.

Whilst the others adjourned to the Cleave Hotel, to do some research into old English ales, I wandered along to the station which was on the Moretonhampstead to Newton Abbot branch line until its closure in 1958. I wanted to see the stone which reads:

"Beneath this slab and laid out flat
    Lies Jumbo, once our station cat."

However, as the station is now a private residence I did not intrude. It was used in the first film version of 'The Hound of the Baskervilles'.

The afternoon session of this circular walk had led certain members of the party to request a more direct route back to Haytor. Despite my suggestions that the straightest line is not always the easiest route, I was put upon by the majority to conform to their edict.

And so it was in jovial spirits that we left the lovely Dartmoor borderland village of Lustleigh to scale the heights past Hisley and

Lustleigh

The Ghost of Jumbo?

Lustleigh

then plummet the depths of the Bovey Valley at the Packsaddle Bridge. The others had insisted on a straighter route and that is exactly what they got. From the Packsaddle Bridge the land rises almost vertically up over Trendlebere Down and then on up again to Black Hill a climb of more than 1100 feet in about a mile. It is not simply a case of statistics for not only is the profile steep but the vegetation is blessed with dense clumps of prickly plants and bushes which can disfigure parts of the anatomy in a way which can cause undue misery. It took us a long time and a lot of bad language to reach the cairn on Black Hill.

Not being of the type to say "I told you so", I joined the others in a much needed rest. The remainder of the walk across the gentle Haytor Down was a pleasant formality. Those poor martyrs soon forgot the trauma of the climb and, rejuvenated, scaled Haytor's well-worn rocks in gay abandon. Needless to say the car park was full of cars and we had a job to find our own vehicle.

Lovely Lustleigh!

10

Best of the Summer Wine—A Vintage Evening Walk from South Brent

Those long days of high summer intensify my passions for walking, a yearning which sees me escape to the hills at the slightest excuse. After a hot and dusty day in the classroom, teaching children who were 'half baked' in more than one sense, my salvation came in the shape of an evening walk. To show no ill feelings I took some of them along to wake them up.

There was definitely no lethargy evident at South Brent, a large moorland village surrounded in hills. After alighting from our coach we made our way freely past the old toll house and along a lovely footpath beside the Avon to Lydia Bridge which spans it.

It was a warm evening suitable for a good stiff stroll without all the encumbrances needed for sterner conditions. Most people sported light packs and there was definitely an air of expectancy as we took the track from the small hamlet of Aish up on to the moor at Ball Gate. This place name prompted one alert individual to ask, why in this part of the moor there were names like Hemerdon Ball, Cuckoo Ball and Corringdon Ball? I told them that balls were rounded hills and there certainly were a lot of balls in this part of the moor.

To wipe the smiles off their faces I led them all quickly up to Three Barrows, a wearisome climb but well worth it, for the views from Ugborough Moor, below and beyond us to the west, were magical as Bodmin Moor was silhouetted against a slowly sinking sun.

I have always felt that the Erme was the loveliest of Dartmoor's rivers but to cross it is another matter. After perilously descending hundreds of feet in only a few minutes it seemed ironical that to cross a flat river it took the group some 15 minutes. I took my boots off and bowled them over to the far bank and then paddled across. Initially it caused me to shriek out loud but it was a most polite shriek because my pupils were around. However, my thoughts on the icy flow and sharp rocks were less pure. I had one quiet chuckle when one of our less agreeable charges went headlong into a deep pool—just reward for all the aggravation he had caused my colleagues and me. Of course I was suitably sympathetic!

A clear track travels south-westwards along the hill beneath

Hillson's House. It enabled us to get to the western side of Burford Down.

At Hall Farm I recounted the story of the infamous Elizabeth Chudleigh (related more fully in Around and About the Haldon Hills) for it was here she grew into a lovely young lady who won the hearts of princes and kings.

Time was on our side, the younger ones keen to use their torches to navigate across the moor in the failing light, so we scaled Hanger Down. By now it was possible to identify certain towns by their lights, Plymouth being particularly noticeable by the great number of them. The most special of all these night time illuminations was one which flashed regularly well out to sea—the Eddystone Light. Having taught the history of the Eddystone that very day I turned to some of those who had endured the lesson and pointed it out to them. I really think they were quite taken with it and looked out to sea in awe and wonder. Less enamoured of the spectacle were a young couple, not of our party, who went unnoticed in the long grass by some of the forerunners of our group, who had the misfortune to trip over them. Very embarrassing!

Fortunately there were no other impediments to cause concern. At Henlake Down the bright lights of Ivybridge lay immediately below us. Going away from us to the A38 was a spectacle worthy of note as westbound traffic was highlighted by red tail lights, whilst oncoming eastward bound traffic was discernible by their headlights.

To reach Ivybridge we took a path and then a road through some extremely dark woodlands down into the town. Stowford Mill resembled a monster, or perhaps it was! On the coach journey home there was much speculation on what the 'Hanger Down lovers' were up to, and sadly the spectacle of the Eddystone Lighthouse hardly got a mention. My theory that the couple were really entomologists carefully studying a rare nocturnal insect was dismissed.

11

From Whiteworks to Walkhampton and Back, Purely for Research

In dawn's first light we turned off the road at Princetown to follow that well made lane south to the end of civilisation at a point

Devonport Leat, The Whiteworks and Foxtor Mires

61

Cuckoo Rock

called the Whiteworks. Ensconced in our battered old passionwagon
were the 'Four Mustgetbeers', all characters of good repute with a
walking pedigree second to none.

The day was set fair with all the potential ingredients required for
an enjoyable excursion across the moors. As we put on our boots,
beneath clear warm skies, we told each other of horrendous tales
from our youth involving the almost legendary Foxtor mires. This is
a gungy morass with featherbeds, quakers and other evil smelling
watery pits ready to accommodate footloose and fancy free walkers
unaware of its dark forbidding presence.

We recalled an outing when an army organised man-hunt resulted
in young troops being sent after us across the moor. They closed in
on us at sunset as we descended Ter Hill but one of our company
knew the dry way over Foxtor mires and the sanctuary of darkness
was enjoyed at the Whiteworks. In the meantime several of the new
recruits acquainted themselves with the soft centre delights of Foxtor mires. We extricated them from their predicament after we had
negotiated a two-hour start the following morning, such was the
extent of their immense gratitude and relief.

Today, we followed the leat to Nun's Cross Farm. The Devonport
leat is full of trout and as we had spied a young boy fishing I
thought policeman Mike was going to caution him in the illegalities

From Sheeps Tor towards Leather Tor

of his piscatorial pursuits but instead he congratulated the boy on his technique and wished him "tight lines"—a term in vogue with fishermen at that time.

We left the leat and followed the lower slopes of Eylesbarrow to visit the rocky Combeshead Tor, a place old Dicky Pengelly knew well as he was the last man to leave the watershed following the building of Burrator Reservoir in 1898. He was allowed to stay on

63

and, living on a diet of rabbits, tobacco and ale, survived a good many years in spartan conditions at Combeshead Farm.

When we got down to Cuckoo Rock, beneath the tor, an argument ensued over who would scramble up to get the box down from the top of the rock. 'Fingers' obliged but the tone of his voice and what it said left one with the distinct impression that it was not an enjoyable experience. 'Willy' just laughed like a pixie the whole time.

We crossed the small combe below Cuckoo Rock and strolled easily up over Yellowmead Down to the impressive Sheeps Tor, a veritable mountain on one side. The scenery around this area, although strongly influenced by man, is impressive. Our only criticism of Sheepstor village was its singular lack of a pub. It merely served to quicken our pace across the great cyclopean dam and up over Yennadon Down to Dousland.

Walkhampton was our destination because at the time I was researching all the pubs in the Dartmoor area for a book I would like to have written called "The Alcoholics Unanimous Guide to Dartmoor Inns". The Walkhampton Inn was one which I needed to sample and I have a vague recollection that the visit was an entirely favourable one.

Walkhampton Church is high on a hill above the village, a fact which was difficult to ignore as we made hard work of struggling up the path to it. My late Uncle Bob's father was a vicar there early in this century. When I was a child he frequently took me to Walkhampton to fish the small stream, a feeder of the Walkham, at the bottom of the hill to the south-east of the church.

Sheeps Tor

We ascended Peek Hill with the others pouring scorn over my claims of 'monster catches' from the diminutive watercourse and the banter lasted to Leather Tor. It was dissolved by the unnerving scramble over the rocks of this hillside pinnacle, popular with postcard and calendar manufacturers because of its pleasing-to-the-eye composition. 'Fingers' added that it was not so pleasant for the feet.

The Devonport Leat provided the ideal corridor to reach open moorland through fragrant conifers. At the aquaduct over the Meavy, 'Fingers', who frequently has amazing brainwaves, suggested that we ought to get a rubber dinghy and sail along the Devonport Leat. The idea was elaborated to include a guitar accompaniment, singing, and some refreshment. If we got bored we could always fish.

Almost fittingly our next port of call was Crazywell Pool. It is supposedly so deep that even if all the bell ropes of Walkhampton Church were tied end to end they would not reach the bottom. Being a non-swimmer I kept well away from this waterfilled disused mine pit. The steep sides provided an excellent spot for a siesta before we took the track back to the Castle Road and anon to the Whiteworks. It was a great surprise to find that we covered as much as 14 miles on such a gentle jaunt which, of course, was done purely for research.

Walkhampton

Where the Devonport Leat plunges into the Meavy Valley

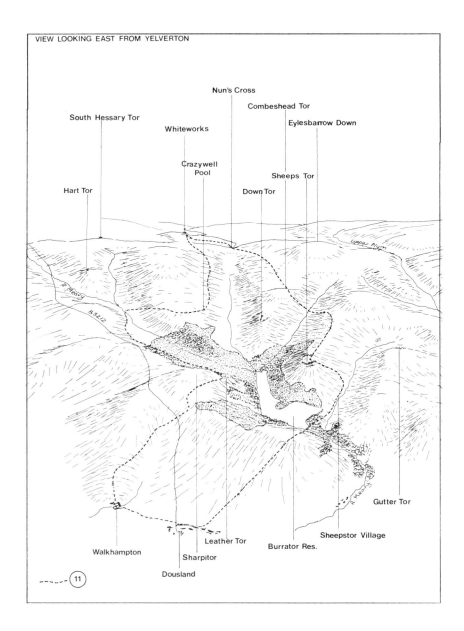

VIEW LOOKING EAST FROM YELVERTON

Nun's Cross

Combeshead Tor

South Hessary Tor

Eylesbarrow Down

Whiteworks

Crazywell
Pool

Sheeps Tor

Hart Tor

Down Tor

Gutter Tor

Sheepstor Village

Walkhampton

Leather Tor

Burrator Res.

Sharpitor

Dousland

11

67

12

The Belstone Renard

We have all read the standard points of advice laid out in all good books about Dartmoor which detail concisely the equipment needed, the preparations, and other fine points to be considered when undertaking an excursion on the moor. However, those guide books do not tell you what to do when a group of French persons turn up hardly equipped to walk across a bowling green leave alone a rugged part of Dartmoor. As leader, in my defence, I had shown this group a graphic set of slides which depicted the necessary equipment, the type of terrain and the unpleasant consequences of not adhering to such advice. But they were French and this seemed sufficient to indemnify them against such traumas, or so they thought . . . Thus *with* a mixture of plimsoles, sandals and various unsuitable articles, and *without* any essential items, we set off on what should have been excellent material for a disaster movie—"Close Encounters of the Miry Kind", or perhaps "Froggies in the Boggies"!

Belstone Stocks—for ill-equipped walkers?

A quick appraisal of their state of dress led to major modifications in the planned route to minimise real risks. Therefore clittery hillsides, venn country and large distances from relative civilisation were cut out. They would get plenty of tracks and, to bring home the realities of Dartmoor walking, at least one bog to dampen their ardour—a sort of gentle package walk.

Enough ramble preamble. At Belstone half the group went for a day-long horse ride whilst the less equine orientated filed out of the village behind me. My limited use of French meant that for me it was to be a fairly quiet sort of day, room to reflect and ruminate on life's mixed blessings.

We climbed past the SWWA offices and onto the open moor on the north-western side of Watchet Hill. As we were entering the firing range, and as I could not remember the French for metal objects, I instructed them not to pick up any nuclear bombs. The more intelligent ones smiled at my lack of vocabulary, the less conversant ones looked very worried.

Fortunately, the weather was dry and sunny as we followed the path to Cullever Steps as an alternative to scrambling over the marvellously rocky pinnacles of Belstone Ridge.

At Scarey Tor we had to wait for a few who had lagged behind. The faster ones occupied themselves by hopping all over the tor. From Cullever Steps we explored the delightful little gorge, which houses the Black-A-Ven Brook, climbing steeply upwards to the artillery road. One or two had shown interest in the moor and I explained some of its facets, notably the army misuse of the moor.

As the ensemble had experienced little discomfort I felt almost duty bound to pixie-lead some of the more ebullient persons into a mire. Between the two branches of the Artillery Road is an uncharted area of exquisite dampness. Within seconds the plaintive cries of "Aidez-moi" (roughly translated as Help!) could be heard from this watery wilderness. The French equivalent of "oh 'eck" was audible on a number of occasions as 'entente cordiale' was tested to its extreme limits. Considering the state some of them got into it seemed safe to assume that they were game for a laugh and went up greatly in my estimation. After this there was no stopping them and they actually began to walk like true walkers and not like something from Ballet Rambert.

The tors seemed to have been a fascination to the French entourage and when asked they gave their assent to the ascent of Row Tor and then West Mill Tor. Although only minor climbs, it indicated an enthusiasm which was appreciated. The third step in this staircase of Dartmoor tors is Yes Tor, the highest tor on Dartmoor. Our French friends voted to give this a miss, even though I pointed out to them that the rock group 'Yes' took their name from this tor, and that on one of their LP's called 'Tormato' it is featured on the sleeve, and the map of the Yes Tor area is featured on the inner sleeve.

Several did not possess a packed lunch or a drink and as Cranmere Pool is not renowned for its wealth of eating houses or take-aways we had to make our way to Okehampton instead.

'Les Renards' near West Mill Tor

An uncomplicated man-made route was followed down past the army camp and beyond to East Hill. From there my preference was the path down to the station followed by a turn to the right down the steep narrow lane towards the lovely Simmons Park, a nerve-racking experience for those without grips on their footwear. The group split up to savour the delights of this busy town and their guide went along to the castle to sightsee. I did not wish to consume any alcoholic substances as to be accused of "being drunk in charge of a group of French students" does not act as a glowing testimonial for future leadership duties.

In mid afternoon the party had finally re-united at the arcade so set off again. Several enquiries were made about the length and duration of the afternoon section and nature of the terrain. I gave

Okehampton Castle

the impression that I thought they wanted a really long walk and apologised that we only had time for about two to three miles. We reached the old mill after a short while and then followed its leat past the main school campus and out of town. The path beneath Ball Hill Quarry and beside the East Okement is through marvellous surroundings. In a few minutes we reached the impressive Fatherford viaduct where, somewhat frantically, the group waved to the passing party of horse riders out for the day. The exchanges were in an excited exuberant way peculiar to the French.

We followed the East Okement southward until we reached a small footbridge. The river hurtles down through this cleave in an alarming fashion, astutely observed by those who knew we had to cross it and could see no apparent bridging point on the map. Overwhelmed with relief, they accepted the steep climb up to Belstone with good humour. The end of their Dartmoor day was a traditional Devonshire cream tea, eaten in an untraditional manner, as one would expect. Once they appreciated just how much jam and cream to put on their scones there was no stopping them and Britain, and Dartmoor in particular, became suddenly a much more amenable place. C'est la vie!

13

A Walkham Walkabout

There are days when one needs to climb up on to Dartmoor where the wind will blow away the cobwebs. Such a day came to us one hot day many years ago.

The journey to the feature known as Devil's Elbow near Princetown was precarious as our conveyance, an old Austin A30, rattled ominously on its maiden voyage under a new skipper. Its only redeeming feature was a Forest Brown sticker in the rear window. The company and the conversation were both good, and intent upon a leisurely examination of a lovely Dartmoor area (and the inside of the inn at Merrivale) we put up with these adversities.

In those days of yore the Devil's Elbow was a dastardly chicane but since then it has been straightened out making a mockery of its name.

Our driver, who had been the target of many wicked remarks, eventually decided to let the relieved offenders out of the baking hot car. In true Dartmoor pixicating fashion we skipped along the former Plymouth and Dartmoor Railway track to the Old Quarries. At this venue 'Bone', one of the quartet, clambered up some precipitous rock faces with apparent ease and without due regard for his own safety or well being. His nickname had been earned by his frequent and spectacular falls leading to fractures to all, or almost all, parts of his anatomy—a good example being a broken arm received after falling off Widgery Cross on Brat Tor.

We found even better chunks of rock at Swell Tor Quarries before getting on with the walk past Criptor and along the track and road down to Ward Bridge. It was really hot as we laboured up to the church at Sampford Spiney. Walking manuals always amplify the way in which it is important to be prepared for inclement weather but always seem to assume that extremely fine weather never occurs on Dartmoor. The intense heat on this occasion had made 'Willy's' face as red as a tomato and a few coatings of cream with a cortisone base did wonders for his comfort, if not his appearance. A big sun hat completed his protective gear which brought strange looks from passersby as we approached Heckwood Tor.

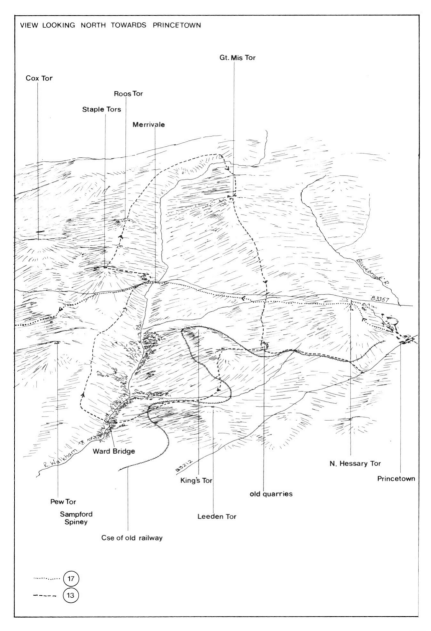

VIEW LOOKING NORTH TOWARDS PRINCETOWN

Gt. Mis Tor

Cox Tor

Roos Tor

Staple Tors

Merrivale

Blackbrook R.

B3357

N. Hessary Tor

Princetown

R. Walkham

Ward Bridge

B3212

King's Tor

old quarries

Pew Tor

Sampford Spiney

Leeden Tor

Cse of old railway

.... 17
- - - - 13

73

Merrivale

We were all duly impressed with Vixen Tor as we got nearer to it. It is the highest tor on Dartmoor on one side, a distinction which 'Bone' had noted with more than a modicum of interest. Fortunately his interest in draught ale was greater in the August heat and we were all grateful to pass on to Merrivale where every parking spot had been taken by other non-climbers. As we had no need of a parking spot we adjourned inside.

After a few pints Mike related the legend of Vixana the wicked witch who lived alone at Vixen Tor in a detached cave. She had the statutory witch like appearance, straggly hair, rotten teeth and a large hooked nose, not unlike one of our party who shall remain nameless! Her party trick was to summon up a mist, when travellers came near, and lure them to a boggy death in Vixen Tor Mire. A young handsome moorman, who had been befriended by pixies, had been given two gifts which would have assured him of immediate membership to the Magic Circle. He could see through the thickest of fogs and, after putting on a ring, could become invisible. Inevitably the confrontation between the wicked witch and the handsome young moorman came about. Despite powerful incantations the witch failed to trap him and flew into an evil rage. The young moorman put on his ring, crept up behind Vixana and

Lesson One—without broomstick!

pushed her over the edge of the tor. As there was no broomstick to hand she fell to her death. The handsome moorman lived the inevitable happy-ever-after life with a beautiful wife. Admittedly the tale sounds a bit better after a few jars.

From Merrivale we climbed up to Roos Tors which is on the top of a truly fine ridge of rocky outcrops. We had wanted to visit Great Mis Tor but the clittery nature of the ground and its steepness led us to traverse Petertavy Great Common and cross the Walkham at a point near Greena Ball. From there we scaled Great Mis Tor where a long siesta ensued, after ensuring the young moorman was not around to push us off.

The route back to Devil's Elbow was unimaginative but easy on the feet because we avoided all upward slopes. Three of us ended with a sun tan whilst 'Willy' still resembled a member of the Munch Bunch.

14

Haytor—'Hippyocracy' and a Dartmoor Salvation

I was an impressionable teenager in those Flower Power years of the 1960s. In those halcyon days a 'hippie happening' was planned for Haytor which I felt would be interesting to attend in order to soak up my fair share of love, peace and the odd bit of granite. I could not afford expensive carillon bells to deck around my neck as a symbol of peace, so made do with some budgie bells acquired from the local pet shop. My hair has always been thin, or fine, so I borrowed my Grandmother's wig. She had a habit of leaving it on the back of the settee and many a time friends had mistaken this for my cat when they had visited our house, and had stroked it fondly for seconds before realising its exact identity.

From Grea Tor looking towards Hound Tor

With a feeling of "goodwill to all men" I set off to Haytor. There were hundreds of folk there, many in deep meditation, others just greasy, foul-mouthed 'drop-outs'. My efforts at trying to talk with several of them failed so miserably that I took off the wig, put on my walking boots (not on my head), and got on with a solo walk to find real peace, beauty and harmony with nature.

This harmony did not stop me getting dampened in the mire near Haytor Quarries but soon after at Grea Tor the warm summer sun dried me out. I had been a little disappointed, even disillusioned, at the aggressive hippies but life still had plenty to offer.

From Grea Tor the view across the upper part of the Becka Brook valley is striking. Hameldown forms an impressive backcloth but noble Hound Tor steals the show with the mysterious Greator Rocks making a lower more unusual step, in a perfect landscape.

Groups of walkers, passed on the way to Hound Tor's medieval village, were noticeably more friendly than my flower and bell sequestered friends of Haytor.

From Hound Tor I made my way stealthily (trespassing) across fields to my favourite little Dartmoor mountain range, that of Chinkwell, Honeybag and Bell Tor. In the many years that have passed by since, I still have not managed to remember which mass of rock applies to each name—a mental block over a granite block.

Hundreds of feet below, in the wide valley of the West Webburn, people could be seen flocking to Widecombe. The dizzy heights of

From Hound Tor to Haytor

Chinkwell had given me an appetite and a zest for greater adventures, but I sat down and went to sleep instead.

It was late afternoon before I finally stirred. There was no rush, nobody and nothing to rush for, and I was feeling happier and healthier than at any time in my life, so charged was I by the beauty of my surroundings. The sunlight was still warm and feeling content I thought that I would take the 'Haytor by-pass' and make my way back to Bovey Tracey (and transport home) through some splendid surroundings.

I made my way down the steep and wet slope towards Hedge Barton. From there I crossed some fields to arrive at Jay's Grave. Cripdon Down in those days was less fenced than of late and was crossed easily so that Hayne Down and the distinctive Bowerman's Nose was reached without too much exertion. The view over the western shoulder of Easton Tor to Kes Tor and Cawsand Hill took the breath away. Though I had gone to Dartmoor to find peace, I had found it in the landscape and not in fellow man, a sort of 'anthropogeomorphological' bond. This great feeling of euphoria manifested itself with a spring in my step that enabled miles to pass by effortlessly.

In a short time I was at the Kestor Inn, Manaton, challenging a bewellingtoned man, of dwarf like proportions, to a game of darts,

Bowerman's Nose (Vawr Maen)

even though I was a real duffer at this game. Naturally I lost quite spectacularly but I had some laughs as this small man could not reach high enough to retrieve his darts when he attempted double twenties and it was amusing to see him jump in hopeful anticipation of getting them back.

The woodlands of the Becka Valley were quite dark but I followed the track to Becky Falls without risk of losing my way. From this deserted beauty spot, several miles of darkening woodlands lay in front of me, but as I was fit I simply ran all the way to the Packsaddle Bridge and on below Gradner Rocks to the Moreton-Newton railway line near Knowle. More running and subsequent trespassing carried me eventually to Southbrook and into the relative metropolis of streetlit Bovey Tracey.

The wait for the last bus back to Exeter was filled with a session at an inn where the landlord took a distinct dislike to my budgie bells. To compensate I had several pints but bemoaned this fact when the Devon General bus took more than an hour to complete the journey to Exeter—the word 'relief' took on a whole new dimension at Exeter bus station.

15

A Safari in the Dartmoor Desert

The most that many people see of Dartmoor is the 'clapped-out' clapper bridge at Postbridge. This involves finding a parking spot as close to the bridge as possible, usually in the large car park, and strolling down to join the masses at the bridge. If only these poor uninitiated people would show a little more adventure, they would discover a Dartmoor far different to the overrated Postbridge.

Having availed ourselves of the facilities, labelled PC on the map, we left Postbridge quickly in a southerly direction, despite the intense summer heat. In Bellever Wood, and apart from a few pesky flies not content to sunbathe and let be, we were soon far from the madding crowd (a good title for a book—I wish I'd thought of it!).

The forest path rises gently away from Postbridge and, after a few hundred feet of climbing, rises even more gently towards

Bellever Tor. The art of forest walking is to know which fork to take when confronted by a choice. Usually it is a straightforward matter of left or right but at times the Forestry Commission like to mischievously create new unchartered thoroughfares which lead into an abrupt dead end after several hundred yards. Take heart, for Bellever is straightforward (at the time of writing) and for our part gave us a pleasant stroll up to the lovely Bellever Tor. The view from this peak is entirely Dartmoor based as peaks, hills and tors rise in all directions. To be able to identify all the landmarks is to know Central Dartmoor comprehensively.

Rather than cut across the forest again we followed its edge to Laughter Tor overlooking the East Dart. Our conversation turned to the merits and demerits of badger gassing. This was prompted by several local recent gassing attempts and the proximity of the home of the well-known badger keeper Ruth Murray who lives on the banks of the Dart.

Having exerted ourselves to the extent that beads of sweat were pouring down our brows, we cooled off by gently strolling down past Huccaby Tor and Ring onto the B3357 road, past Pixieland and Pixie's Holt to Dartmeet. We had expected there to be a lot of people but were amazed by the half-mile tail-back up Dartmeet hill as we entered this cauldron of heat. It was so hot that people were lying in the river to cool off, and ice creams were melting instantly. There was a profusion of knotted handkerchiefs on heads.

The climb up to Yar Tor is gruelling, even with a chill winter wind to refresh but under these conditions it was almost impossible. On no less than five occasions did we have to stop to "look at the view"—a quaint expression invoked when the hill is too steep for walkers and a brief respite is necessary to revive flagging spirits. We all knew the score as we encouraged some of the less fit members of our troop. By tolerance and good humour we managed to keep going to the top and then rested for some time on Yar Tor's summit.

Distant Princetown shimmered like a mirage, the tall mast appearing to waver. Hundreds of feet below us holidaymakers, day trippers and coach passengers looked like little ants. A long queue was visible into the 'ladies' which seemed strange in this heat as we had downed gallons of orange squash and there was no hint of a dash behind a rock for us!

Postbridge

This particular part of the moor is strikingly beautiful. To get the best of the views we passed the sad memorial to a lost soldier, who was killed at the tender age of nineteen, to reach the summit of Corndon Tor.

This is a great tor with extensive views. The others thought I was crazy to sit and pan around all the different horizons snapping away at the colourful moors. I knew that the photographs I took would rekindle these magic moments of high summer when looking back on stormy winter nights never too far off.

Our initial idea had been to visit Hameldown's giant hump, via Shallowford, but the great heat would have fried us alive had we been foolish enough to scale such dizzy heights so commonsense prevailed.

We made our way to Sherwell and then on to the ancient tenement of Babeny where the Walla Brook was barely more than a trickle. We found a deep pool and wallowed in it for a long while until we dragged ourselves along the east bank of the East Dart to Bellever.

The weatherman said that this would be one of the hottest days of

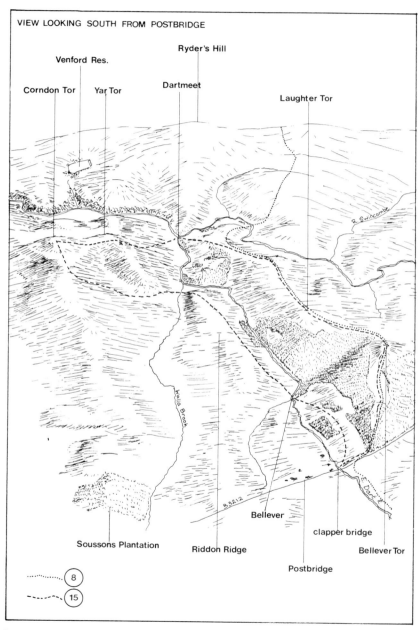

VIEW LOOKING SOUTH FROM POSTBRIDGE

Ryder's Hill

Venford Res.

Corndon Tor   Yar Tor   Dartmeet

Laughter Tor

R. Swincombe

Wella Brook

B.3212

Bellever

clapper bridge

Soussons Plantation   Riddon Ridge   Bellever Tor

Postbridge

8
15

82

the century, the heat haze on the road to Postbridge reinforced this notion. Although we had only mastered about nine miles this had been sufficient to inflict great tiredness and even more lethargy than usual. The inside of our car was so hot that we had to leave doors and windows open for a full half hour before getting in for the long journey home. After all, having been fried on the walk we didn't wish to be baked on the way home! Despite the discomfort of the high temperatures this was a truly marvellous stroll in the heartland of Dartmoor, a day when even pesky flies eventually gave up the hunt and went to sunbathe on the clapper bridge at Postbridge.

16

To Ducks' Pool via Heaven!

September is a magical month for Dartmoor walking. Often an Indian summer brings unmitigated delight to early mornings where mists fill the valleys and the hilltops appear like islands up in the heavens. For us such a day came following a late night of revelry when gallons of Newcastle Brown ale were consumed. Therefore the morning glory was tinged with a touch of drowsiness as we emerged from our vehicle at Cross Furzes (above Buckfastleigh) at an hour when even the larks still awaited the call of their alarm clocks.

In the first mile of lane walking up to Lud Gate there was little to see as the morning mist was cool, damp and clinging. On our outward journey to Dartmoor we had glimpsed occasional views of peaks protruding above the mists and in our hearts hoped that we would soon attain them. However, ahead of us lay Puper's Hill, an unrelenting hill of sharp incline, enough to knock the stuffing out of most walkers on the first mile of a new pilgrimage.

Great excitement arose, just above Lud Gate, as it was apparent we were emerging above the clouds and that we had at last made it up to Heaven! Stretched for miles away below us was a blanket of cloud, fortunately devoid of cherubims and seraphims—not a single harp in sight. A desperate rush followed to reach the summit of Puper's so that we could survey this wondrous scene. The cloud

cover was at about a thousand feet above sea level, but presumably this was not a constant level because the far off Haldon Hills (circa 800 feet a.s.l.) could be spied like islands in a sea of mist. Bewitched and beguiled by the splendour of it all we sat for many minutes, gazing silently in awe at this spectacle. High up on Puper's Hill we were in a Kingdom of warmth and birdsong, whilst way below us was a world of grey. We enjoyed our role as overlords and some of our disciples questioned whether or not what we were experiencing had anything to do with the hallucinatory brew of brown ale consumed the previous night. A dull explanatory narrative about such geophysical theories as the adiabatic lapse rate confusingly but soberly convinced them that it was a meteorological phenomenon and not one induced by over indulgence.

The exploration of our 'island world' necessitated that we should travel 'inland' just north of Huntingdon Warren towards Aune or

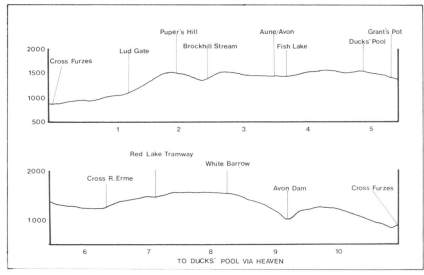

Avon Head. The dry autumn weather was ideal for such a journey as the headwaters of this marvellous Devonshire river are notoriously wet and in the winter they are worth avoiding. At its wicked worst Aune Head can cause immense discomfort with a baptism of the kneecaps virtually assured for any perambulist intent on a speedy crossing of this watery wilderness. In such a featureless and damp environment tin miners, 'the old men' of Dartmoor, extracted a tough living, but now their days are long gone. The evidence of their endeavours are all too apparent across the whole of Dartmoor. We visited the remains of the former tinners' huts at Fish Lake.

Here a letterbox, set in monotonously dull and stark surroundings, distracted us for a while but in warm bright sunlight the urge was strong to reach Ducks' Pool for an extremely early lunch. We traversed Green Hill to reach a shrine there set up to honour William Crossing, a celebrated Dartmoor explorer, journalist and author. Appropriately, as we walked we discussed his literary offerings, and although many champion his 'Guide to Dartmoor', we were unanimous that his most readable book is 'Amidst Devonia's Alps' which captures the flavour of the moor and his love for it. Books that instruct walkers on potential routes tend to remove the sense of adventure or fun at self-discovery. However, for many people they fulfill a self assuring need and are usually most informative, though they tend to make dull reading.

Ducks' Pool, Southern Dartmoor's equivalent of Cranmere Pool, is a shallow depression with more mire than water. A large rock bears the commemorative plaque to Mr Crossing. It is far easier to reach Ducks' Pool than Cranmere as there are some extremely well worn tracks that skirt the mires and morasses in this part of the moor. Later we used one of them, called Black Lane, to follow the stream southwards towards Stringers Hill. A few hundred yards above the confluence of the two streams are more industrial archaeological remnants from the days of pioneer mining. A hole in the ground, probably used for shelter or storage purposes, bears the name Grant's Pot. It was not surprising to discover another letterbox there.

At the river bank we found a marvellous sun trap where we slept for a generous hour or so. Dartmoor dreams are always better and the rest was much appreciated, an oasis in a period of intense activity. We were so secluded that we heard the laughter of passing

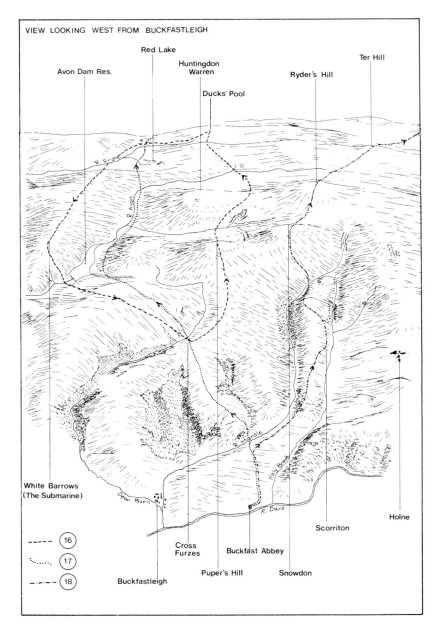

VIEW LOOKING WEST FROM BUCKFASTLEIGH

Red Lake

Avon Dam Res.

Huntingdon
Warren

Ter Hill

Ryder's Hill

Ducks' Pool

White Barrows
(The Submarine)

Holne

Scorriton

- - - - - (16)

.... (17)

-.-.-.- (18)

Cross
Furzes

Buckfast Abbey

Buckfastleigh

Puper's Hill

Snowdon

86

walkers closeby. It is unlikely that they suspected there were four Rip Van Winkles enjoying almost total oblivion a few yards away.

The elixir of sleep worked as a great tonic. Apart from a few minutes spent in splashing enormous amounts of the River Erme at each other, the rest of the walk was full of rigorous action. We crossed the Erme and struck up a strong walking rhythm over Crossways and up to Petre's Cross. Ahead of us 'the submarine' loomed large. For the uninitiated this is an obvious nickname for White Barrows owing to its distinct nautical shape.

It was noticeable that we were no longer an island race as South Devon had returned to a world of sunlight, although undoubtedly that night it would again be enshrined within another enveloping mist. Throughout this book I have sung the praises of views from many elevated bastions because they are so memorable and the view from White Barrows was no exception. Up periscopes! There is probably no other point in Devon from which you can see so many miles to the south, east and west. Raymond Cattell, one of the world's leading psychologists, said of this vantage point, "It is indeed a great place for a chair of philosophy"—albeit a trifle hard!

Topographical philosophy dictates that what goes down must unfortunately go up again. And so it was that we descended to the Avon Dam and immediately climbed over the down above known as Smallbrook Plains. It always seems a strange contradiction of terminology that you always have to go up to reach a down. To compensate we went down over Lambs Down, traversed a shadowy Dean Burn and returned to Cross Furzes, a spiritually richer group for the journey—about 11 miles and about 20 winks.

The Abbot's Way

Traditionally the first Sunday in October is set aside by groups ‹ walkers for the annual pilgrimage known as the Abbot's Way. The walk of about 25 miles, organised by the Tavistock Youth and Community College, raises much needed funds for the Dartmoor Rescue Group. Historically it is based on a supposed ancient route across the moor between Buckfast and Tavistock Abbeys. Another track formerly branched off to Buckland Abbey to allow 'jobbers' to carry their merchandise, largely fleeces, across the moor on pack-horses. The route is not necessarily exactly as shown on the map and certainly it is different to the one chosen for this Abbot's Way walk.

We were five teams, of four to eight members in each, and before we could embark on this stroll we had to pass through a semi-rigorous check-out where stewards examined our kit and essential accessories to see that we were suitably equipped to tackle this

A 'Mass' exit from Buckfast?

WE SELL.

CHALKS PENS PENCILS.
GLUE SELLOTAPE.STRING.
DRAWING PINS.COTTON.
NEEDLES.CRIPS.COMBS.PINS.
PLAYING CARDS. LICHT BULBS.
CANDLES.FUSES FUSE WIRE.
POLISH.SHOE LACES. BOOKS.
SAFETY PINS. STATIONARY.
TOOL SET.TOYS.HATS. MAPS.
BATTERIES.BIRTHDAY.CARDS.
POSTCARDS.HONEY.SWEETS.
GROCERIES.GREENGROCERIES.
CLOTTED CREAM.MINERALS.
ICE CREAM.CIGARETTES.FILMS.
CLOTHES PEGS.FLOOR CLOTHES.
DISH CLOTES.FLANNELS.TIGHTS.
TOILETRIES.MOTTO BOARDS.
GIFTS. BAGS.

potentially arduous stroll. There was no pulling the wool over their eyes—if you will excuse the play on words.

At the appointed hour of nine o'clock several hundred walkers set off from Buckfast. In our ranks we had a couple of Australian guests who we promptly dubbed 'The Cobbers Jobbers' because of their ability to spin a good yarn. In less than a hundred yards we saw the sign as shown in the photograph. A polite enquiry about the purchase of a kitchen sink was met with an equally quaint old fashioned glare.

The throng, who were soon into their stride, were in good and somewhat heady spirits. The instructions to the walkers were that they should be fairly silent on the hallowed territory of Buckfast as the Abbot was celebrating mass that morning—thus as soon as they were away, following a mass exit, noisy excitement reigned supreme.

The steepness of the seemingly never-ending road section up to Cross Furzes soon realised the stony silence again as breath was required for walking.

Although this is not a race, several groups could be seen dis appearing over the sky line in great haste. In front of them at relatively supersonic speeds, the Dark Peak fraternity, and other fell runners like them, disappeared in a cloud of dust. These persons treat a stroll like the Abbot's Way almost with contempt. On a past walk we met one at Princetown at lunch time and jokingly accused him of slacking. His stone-faced reply was that he had finished the walk an hour previous and was on his way back to Buckfast!

Sheepishly climbing over Lambs Down

Our own humble efforts continued beyond Cross Furzes as we descended a lane to cross the delightful Dean Burn. The struggle over the edge of the aptly named Lambs Down created a few puffs and pants, but generally the fine views across the moor and South Hams compensated for the discomfort. The temptation to stop for a brief respite was more than ameliorated by the desire to reach Princetown by lunch time so that we could continue our research into listed buildings which served alcoholic substances. Accordingly we had deemed it necessary to commit to paper a rigid schedule which reached Princetown at about 1.30 pm.

We were so calculating that we almost forgot to appreciate the lovely Avon valley and reservoir below us to the south-west. One of the 'Cobbers Jobbers' enquired whether or not this 'little oasis' was man made.

Brockhill Ford was crossed without any bother as the well-marked way followed the Avon or Aune Valley north-westwards opposite the unlikely sounding Bishop's Meads. The river was crossed dryly but several of the pilgrims succumbed to wet feet in a bog beyond the river banks. Following the Avon had given us a false sense of security as the ground was relatively flat. By rude contrast the climb up to Crossways, and another checkpoint, reminded us that Dartmoor is a rugged and energy-sapping moor. If the steep hills do not tire you, long grass or heavily saturated ground will—you certainly can't win (unless you are very fit).

This pessimistic philosophy endured as we skirted the swamps of Red Lake mire to pick up the remaining vestiges of that loveliest of Devon rivers, the Erme. After some initial harrassment from boggy terrain we made good ground towards Broad Rock (which isn't).

An odd incident happened at this remote point. On our approaches we had seen the distinctive white police helicopter hovering over the moor and had jokingly quipped that perhaps a prisoner had escaped from Princetown Prison and the police thought that it was one of us. Imagine our surprise when we saw two of our group, a father and son, being airlifted. It later transpired that a member of their family had been rushed to hospital. Fortunately we later learned that she was recovering after a knock on the head and all was well.

There was nothing that we could do other than carry on in haste just to the west of Great Gnats Head on a bee line for Nun's Cross

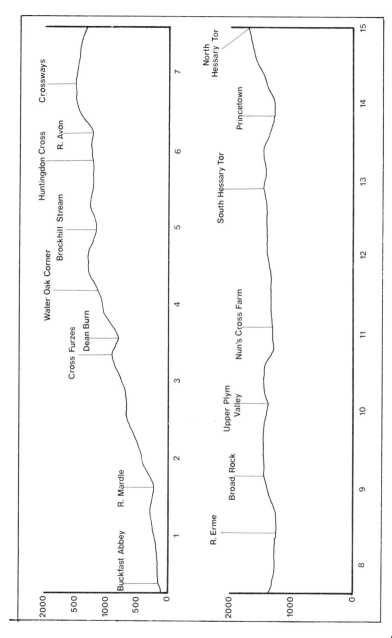

Farm. Being a pedestrian thinker it suddenly dawned on me just how many religious place names we had passed that morning, almost sufficient to work the route out without any secular guidance from the OS maps. We had passed Cross Furzes, Dean Moor, Bishop's Meads, Huntingdon Cross, Crossways to reach Nun's Cross Farm.

The pendulum of flagging/soaring spirits got a boost when we breezed past Peat Cot in rejuvenated fashion as we had got ahead of our schedule. We reassured the company that at Princetown we would rest for an hour and that after lunch the completion of the last seven miles or so would be a mere formality. The correct term for this is 'kidology'.

Although it was possible to follow the road into Princetown (known as the Castle Road) we elected to take the more authentic route via South Hessary Tor.

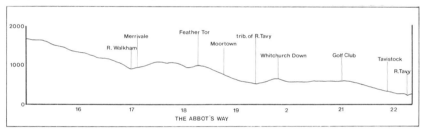

In England's highest town a prolonged rest was enjoyed. Some of us availed ourselves of the facilities on offer at the various hostelries, whilst several others collapsed in our coach which had made the long detour around the moor to meet us for a lunchtime rendezvous. One lad had enough surplus energy to go looking for the remains of Princetown station. Despite only finding one railway sign, threatening a forty shillings fine or extermination, he was quite ecstatic at this festering trove of railway memorabilia. My friends and I had thoughts along other lines.

Being the overall leader of our group, the task fell on my young shoulders to whip up the necessary response to raise the ensemble for the last charge. There were the dubious, suspicious and sceptical who were won over by the ploy that, apart from one big hill, the rest of the walk was merely a pleasant stroll with some tremendous views. No mention was made of the sustained effort required to attain these vistas!

92

VIEW LOOKING EAST FROM TAVISTOCK

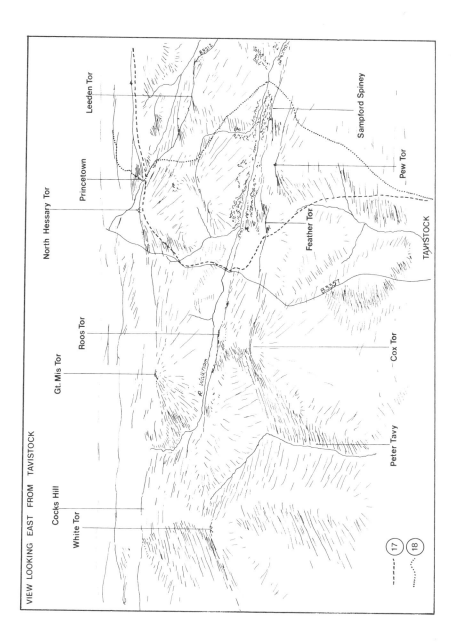

White Tor

Cocks Hill

Gt. Mis Tor

Roos Tor

North Hessary Tor

Princetown

Leeden Tor

Sampford Spiney

Pew Tor

Feather Tor

Cox Tor

Peter Tavy

TAVISTOCK

B3212

B3357

R. Walkham

17
18

93

And so it was a little lightheaded, and a lot less thirsty, that we made the ascent of North Hessary Tor. One of our Australian friends said that the view, in his opinion, was "out of this world". He said this while gazing beyond the pastoral lands, to the south of Bodmin Moor, to the white spoil mountains of the St Austell China Clay pits. Another colleague warned him that such remarks might be misinterpreted by stalwart Cornishmen! The great William Crossing is also known to have held the view from North Hessary in high esteem. From such an elevated spot the only way to travel is downhill and after so many miles nobody seemed opposed to the few relatively easy miles down to Merrivale and across the Walkham River.

Past baptisms in the boggy area just to the north-west of Vixen Tor were sufficient to prompt us to skirt it by remaining on the main road for an extra few hundred yards, before we headed off to Feather Tor Cross, one of many religious markers on the route. The remainder of the route probably would not whet the appetite of the ardent moorman because it is a mixture of lanes, commons and roads, but for me, the gentle gradients and open views across the rich landscape are worth savouring.

Our team of wayfarers had by now reached various stages of wear and tear. Some looked pale and drawn, whilst others were ominously

TAVISTOCK AND DISTRICT
YOUTH AND COMMUNITY SERVICES COMMITTEE

Certificate

Awarded to

D. J. Hill

for
Abbots Way Walk

-5. OCT. 1980

Adrian Bewell Chairman
T.D.Y.C.S.C.

fit and looked capable of doing another twenty-five miles. Those with blisters looked the most uncomfortable and, alas, I was one of that fraternity as I walked with one boot on and one off across the edge of Tavistock Golf Course on Whitchurch Down. In a decidedly hobbledy-hoy fashion we merrily trundled down into Tavistock. The evidence of our labours on this absolutely marvellous walk were visible in our cherished certificates, and in the great number of our company who enjoyed a blissfully deep sleep on the coach journey home.

18

New Habits—the other Abbot's Way

They say old habits die hard, and having completed several official Abbot's Way walks, I felt the urge to tread new ground between the starting and finishing points. An opportunity arose as my walking club had about thirty entries and being 'surplus to requirements' I opted to take a small group another way.

Uphill lane walking took us up to Scorriton—there was no hint of life. The lane from Scorriton up to the moor could easily be classified as the motorway of Dartmoor tracks. In places it is far wider than either of the B roads which cross Dartmoor and certainly much straighter. We laboured upwards with the panoramas increasing correspondingly. At one gateway where we paused to savour the view, and recapture our breath, we noticed that two small flat concrete blocks, either side of the gate, were inscribed 'G PoW' and '1946'. Our computer-like brains immediately interpreted this as a German Prisoner of War who, in 1946 had left his mark on the Devon countryside. We didn't think it strange that he should write it in English. Other less successful attempts were noted higher up the lane.

Above Scorriton

From Snowdon looking down the valley of the R. Mardle. A-R Mardle; B-Scorriton Down; C-Hembury Fort; D-Buckfast; E-Track to Chalk Ford; X-marks 'No Entry'

At Scorriton Down we were shocked to discover that the well-defined track to our right was closed to walkers. A notice suggested the owners would take trespassers to task for any infringement. This was especially upsetting for we had planned to utilise this thoroughfare to take us onto the open moor to join the Sandy Way. It simply re-inforces the notion that OS maps would do well to indicate positive (or is it negative?) no-go areas so that route planning could be more accurate.

Cursing and muttering we descended to Chalk Ford bemoaning the fact that having climbed several hundred feet, slowly, we had to descend in order to climb back to the same level. Chalk Ford has its compensations being a lovely sheltered spot, and boasts a neat footbridge to facilitate a dry crossing of the sparkling, but little known, River Mardle. This stream tumbles steeply down through woods and fields to Buckfastleigh where it has a confluence with the River Dart near the start of the Dart Valley Railway.

From Chalk Ford we struggled through chest-high ferns and gorse upwards towards Snowdon. This energy-draining exercise was punctuated by a few brief stops to take off outer clothing layers, in the warm early October sunshine. This corner of the moor affords truly magnificent views. This was the case particularly towards the eastern moor with the scenery spanning from Rippon across to Corndon Tors. We were in no rush and sat down at the top of tin workings near Snowdon to survey the moors and South Devon over a sandwich and a well earned drink, walking at its best.

Ryder's Hill is the highest point on the southern moor which is reached by a gentle, but damp, climb from Snowdon. My old camera attempted to capture the wide vista but with a fixed lens had to do it by instalments.

Our lunchtime destination, Princetown, could be seen boldly ahead of us, but I knew the apparent short distance to it was false, full of miry horrors and subsequent Anglo-Saxon phraseology. This started instantly within fifty yards of Ryder's Hill trig point, when one of the crew suddenly performed unintentional acrobatics before landing in an undignified way. Unscathed, apart from pride, the person picked himself up and promptly did the same unnerving manoeuvre again on Ter Hill.

An old view of the Castle Road into Princetown

To cross the Swincombe River we descended to the small reservoir below Ter Hill. To get to the river we really had to struggle over the most difficult ground. Beyond it the lower slopes of Royal Hill were a pleasant contrast. We marched to Tor Royal and I ran on to Princetown to beat Last Orders—the secular and not spiritual ones.

It is a sensible philosophy to do the lions share of a walk before a prolonged rest, as psychologically it is easier to gird up ones loins if the remainder of a walk is not too daunting.

From Princetown we followed the course of the former Plymouth and Dartmoor Railway. As we gathered steam we passed a middle-aged couple, ill-equipped for a safari, at a point where the old railway bridge had been removed. The lady challenged me by asking

An old view of the Plymouth and Dartmoor Railway which closed in 1956

how much further they had to go before they found the stone railway lines, "as seen some years ago on Clive Gunnell's Dartmoor TV programme." Alas, the poor lady was confused, for it was at distant Haytor that this line once operated. We continued along the track for a short while before dropping down to Criptor, on a bee-line for Ward Bridge spanning the River Walkham.

The remainder of the walk past Sampford Spiney and along Whitchurch Down was largely by road. For most of the way the open down and golf course permitted us to walk beside the road towards Tavistock. We were amused by a couple of ancient golfers who seemed to have great difficulty in hitting the ball straight. We counted that one player had about 18 shots before sinking the ball in the hole, hopefully the right one.

Beyond the golf course we entered prosperous Tavistock, ancient stannary town, cultural centre of the central Tavy valley. With historic blisters to boot we limped into Tavistock School, only to be greeted by our colleagues with "What kept you?"

19

New Boots, New Blisters and New Bridge

It was November, but only just. That annual debacle, my birthday, had been acknowledged by an expensive pair of new walking boots. Never before had so much been spent on a present for me,

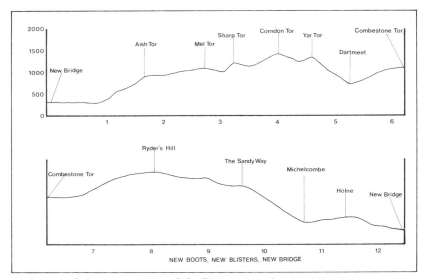

Top chart labels:
2000, 1500, 1000, 500, 0

New Bridge, Aish Tor, Mel Tor, Sharp Tor, Corndon Tor, Yar Tor, Dartmeet, Combestone Tor

1 2 3 4 5 6

Combestone Tor, Ryder's Hill, The Sandy Way, Michelcombe, Holne, New Bridge

7 8 9 10 11 12

NEW BOOTS, NEW BLISTERS, NEW BRIDGE

so I was duly most grateful. Being 'au fait' with the necessary formalities of breaking in boots, well in advance of any walk, I put them on each night and even wore them in bed (my wife's bruises were testimony to this erotic bedtime wear) for a full fortnight before this walk.

Thus, with my feet entombed within a pair of heavy leather coffins, or so it felt, my friends and I set forth from an unusually quiet New Bridge. We walked westwards beside the Dart, on its north side, following level ground for almost a mile. This at least gave me a brief opportunity to see what walking in real boots could be like. Because I really wanted to test them fully, like one of those adverts on television, I splashed through puddles, scaled unnecessary obstacles, tried some sprinting, backwards walking and other

Sharp Tor as seen from the side of Corndon. A-Sharp Tor; B-Venford Reservoir; C-Holne Ridge

A   B   C

manoeuvres. The end result of such thoughtless gay abandon was that I was semi-fatigued at the bottom of the steep hill up to Aish Tor whilst the others were perfectly primed for the ascent.

In the next half a mile we climbed about six hundred feet, an average gradient of about 20 per cent (1:5) for fifteen minutes.

By sharp contrast the gently curving track, above Hockinston Tor, to Mel Tor, enabled us all to regain our feeling of fitness, although it is fair to say that the view of the Dart Gorge below us was enough to take our breath away—at least in a metaphoric sense. This spectacular valley, with its precipitously steep lower wooded slopes, and its rocky outcropped shoulders, is one of Dartmoor's greatest treasures. To walk in the valley bottom can be almost impossible at times, but to view it from Sharp Tor or, even better, Bench Tor is to see it at its best. In its autumn glory it was pure golden magic.

This communion with the landscape ceased at Sharp Tor. A keen wind necessitated that we use one of its giant boulders as a wind break whilst we had a coffee break high up in our aerie, a rocky cathedral of Dartmoor granite.

Our quota for the day was about a dozen miles so we lavished a few on the twin masses of Corndon Tor and Yar Tor. The former has always been a favourite of mine because of its lofty gaze into Eastern Dartmoor, a land of 'grockle traps' but of immense beauty.

We turned our backs on this panorama to descend sharply to Dartmeet where there was not a single knotted handkerchief in sight. With such a lack of cars and coaches it was possible to appreciate the loveliness of Dartmeet for it was not obscured by people in the chilly November breeze.

Ahead of us lay an enormously long climb up to Ryder's Hill, the highest point, at 1696 feet, on the southern moor. Being masters of guile at route planning, we cleverly stage-managed it so that the ascent, which approached a thousand foot climb, was done in sections. The initial onslaught enabled us to scale Combestone Tor in a short sharp burst. Once on this fine tor we sat out of the wind to enjoy our lunch. It is always grand to dine at elevated locations.

Afterwards we made our way along the leat leading up the hidden valley of the O or Wo Brook. My walking rhythm was impeded by a distinct rubbing in my right heel which made me believe that the boots had not been sufficiently 'bedded'. An unscheduled stop saw

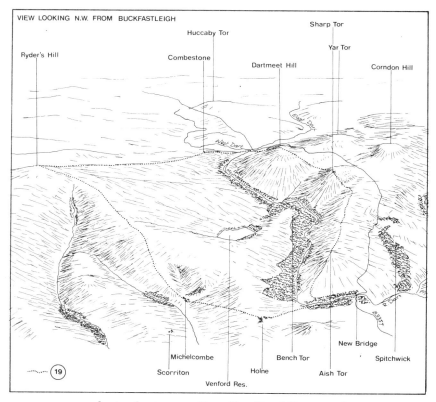

VIEW LOOKING N.W. FROM BUCKFASTLEIGH

Ryder's Hill · Huccaby Tor · Combestone · Dartmeet Hill · Sharp Tor · Yar Tor · Corndon Hill

West Dart

19

Michelcombe · Scorriton · Venford Res. · Holne · Bench Tor · Aish Tor · New Bridge · Spitchwick

an enormous elastoplast cover the offending blister and a temporary respite of pain was enjoyed up to the trig point on Ryder's Hill. For posterity the old camera was taken out to capture the view. Normally I specialise in masterful photos of thumbs and lens caps but today I managed to actually get some of the scenery into the photograph!

Ryder's Hill is typical of most of the hills in this area of Dartmoor lacking in rocky outcrops to identify it. Amongst other hills in the area which fall into this category are Nakers Hill, Green Hill, Ter and Skir Hill. From this high point there was only one possible way to go and that was downhill. The Sandy Way is well marked across the moor and provided us with a marvellous exit from open moorland. The immense views across South Devon were fully enjoyed because the easy terrain beneath our feet did not distract us. The three miles to the hamlet of Michelcombe only took forty minutes, even with troublesome blisters—a descent of a thousand feet.

The rest of the trek was a formality. Holne was apparently closed for the winter so we maintained a fast pace along the public footpath down through the woods and back to New Bridge.

Although the boots were continually worn for weeks afterwards they never relented and for almost their entire life gave me a hard time. It was only when they were well worn did they begin to fit and then it was time to replace them.

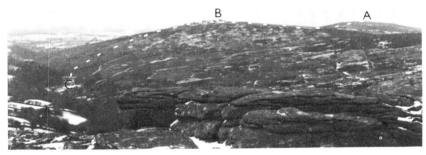

At Combestone Tor (A) Corndon Tor; (B) Yar Tor; (C) Dartmeet

20

Throwleigh to Warren House in the Wet Monsoon Season

Installed within our luxury superchug bus we turned off the A30 at South Zeal and took the narrow twisting road towards Throwleigh. The unsuspecting driver could be seen to be not entirely happy at the difficult manoeuvres necessary to negotiate the narrow lanes to Ensworthy. At this point he was able to turn his coach around. We got off to prepare for our stroll across to the Warren House Inn.

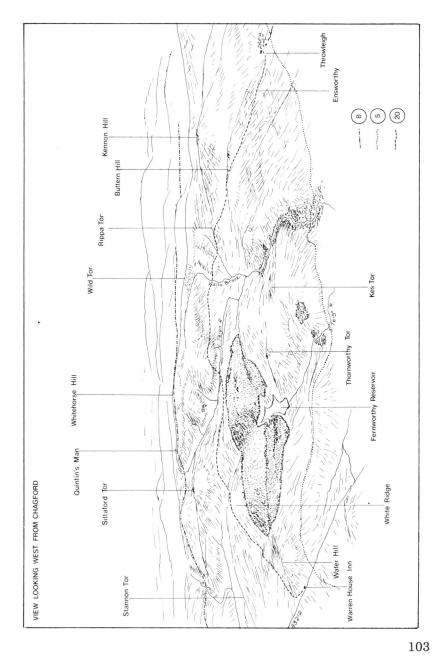

VIEW LOOKING WEST FROM CHAGFORD

Stannon Tor

Sittaford Tor

Quintin's Man

Whitehorse Hill

Wild Tor

Rippa Tor

Buttern Hill

Kennon Hill

Throwleigh

Ensworthy

Walla Brook

Kes Tor

Thornworthy Tor

Fernworthy Reservoir

White Ridge

Water Hill

Warren House Inn

8

5

20

103

It is always puzzling to observe that several people will sit on the coach for an hour wondering how long it will be before we arrive at our destination and then take about 15 minutes to put on their boots and walking clothes. This ritualistic delay encourages observers to retie boots more tightly, unwrap boiled sweets, jump up and down, stare knowingly at the map or sit down and start on their packed lunches. For my part, I ignore all questions as to the nature of the terrain to be traversed, and get on with donning my boots and walking clothes! I don't mention the miry hollows or never ending steep slopes as that would deflate their morales. Here is the log of events that befell us after we left Ensworthy on that late Autumn day.

We followed the rough track up to the open moor at Buttern Hill. Cautiously aware that this area of the moor boasts such dire mires as Gidleigh Common, Gallaven and Ruelake Pit, we skirted the former to reach the spur of Rippator or Rival Tor. This is one of the few masses on Dartmoor to be named on the OS map with two names. We had with us one or two newcomers to Dartmoor walking who were visibly puffing and panting, so we sat down awhile to let them recuperate. For the inquisitive members of our troop we identified the higher peaks like Watern Tor, Wild Tor and Steeperton and also showed them the distant Kes Tor.

When I showed them the route we were due to follow they all seemed mystified that we had not gone across the low-lying Gidleigh Common. Poor uninitiated ramblers! Gidleigh Common is wetter underfoot than the rivers which pass through it. Even the banks of the North Teign River, below Shovel Down, can be a daunting prospect although at least the bed of the river is solid.

We travelled southwards keeping to high ground, once we had crossed the Gallaven Brook. The terrain as far as Walla Brook enabled us to get into a good stride, but beyond it the long vegetation on the lower side of Watern Tor meant hard going. Bogs, boulders and long grasses accounted for much of the stumblingly slow progress.

The North Teign has its own mini-gorge beneath Hew Down and Manga Hill. The river drops steeply through it in fine fashion providing a sheltered spot from the prevailing westerlies in splendid surroundings. By popular request we stopped for several minutes in this sheltered hollow. As we scanned the moor many tiny dots could be seen in the distance. As they got closer it dawned on us that these were the masochistic runners who go out on the moor for a two day expedition which is held at different venues each year. Consequently they travelled light with shorts worn over tights or track suit bottoms. These pseudo-Supermen breathlessly competed with each other and, despite their pained expressions, no doubt enjoyed Dartmoor in their own inimitable way. When we crossed the footbridge near Teign Head Farm a swarm of them appeared out of the mist and shot into Fernworthy Forest with impressive ease. We also climbed up Long Ridge but altered course onto the track up to Grey Wethers.

With the rain falling heavily and obliquely straight into our faces it was not long before we were thoroughly drenched. I was particularly upset by such a comprehensive soaking as I had invested in a reputed top-name weather-proof garment that in

reality offered little resistance to the elements. On top of White Ridge I dipped into a 'sealed' pocket only to find that my extra strong mints had been eroded by the rainwater and my fingers met a soggy mess.

To compensate for these miseries we made a bee-line for the Warren House Inn. Normally we would have skirted the awful bogs that lie in a direct line between White Ridge and the Warren House but, as we could get no wetter, it seemed fitting to simply plough through all the mud and mire. At the Warren House we dried out as best we could. I stuck my head for several minutes under the hot air hand drier (so much more efficient than roller towels) and then made good use of the stereo open fires in an attempt to dry the rest of me. The good company and ale helped to alleviate the mornings shortcomings. The group unanimously voted not to walk any further—the boxing equivalent of throwing in the much needed towel.

--------------------------- **21** ---------------------------

The Tavy Cleave and Rattlebrook—via Peking

Travel with Clive and there will never be a dull moment. Not only will he entertain you with a barrage of bizarre events, amusing anecdotes and jokes, but he will almost certainly convey you to your destination in the most roundabout way imaginable. Today was typical as we had agreed where to park and explore but, so enthused was he with his narrative that, instead of taking the A30 Exeter to Okehampton road, we found ourselves heading south-westwards along the A38. This misdirection was so confidently executed that I almost believed he knew a secret route that the motoring authorities had failed to identify. Our journey thus took us a lot longer and further as we involuntarily visited such exotic places as Bovey Tracey, Moretonhampstead and Sandy Park as we weaved across Devon.

Later than planned we donned our boots, garments and packs at the Dartmoor Inn near Lydford. This splendid walking area is prone to the prevailing westerlies, as the open country across to Bodmin

Approaching the Tavy Cleave

Moor allows the wind to gather momentum as it serges up to north-western Dartmoor. Today the full fury of the elements blew us to a crossing place on the Lyd at High Down (which is a low down). The words 'crossing place' may conjure up the image of evenly spaced stepping stones, but in reality the crossing was a stumbling, unco-ordinated affair which rendered my right boot full of icy cold water. The worst thing about my waterproof boots is that they fail to let water out once it has got in! This moist point is not one readily aired in the sales patter of boot purveyors. By the time we got to White Hill the water had warmed up and we rubbed our hands with glee at the prospect of entering our favourite Dartmoor canyon, the Tavy Cleave.

To reach this Utopian valley we followed the Reddaford Leat which contours the hill below Nat Tor. 'Cleave' is a derivative of 'cliff' found also at other places on the moor, notably at Lustleigh Cleave and Belstone Cleave. Its immense beauty has lured many folk to camp beside the Tavy's fast flowing waters only to be engulfed by overnight floods and many have lost their lives there. The Tavy has many tributaries, all rise on the high ground of Northern Dartmoor which experiences vast amounts of rainfall. In storms the surface run-off swells the Tavy so swiftly that it rises many feet in a few hours. Whilst the "Dart may well claim your heart", the "Tavy will put you in your gravey"! The cascade at a small waterfall was so noisy that it actually silenced Clive!

The appeal of the Tavy Cleave is its precipitous and rocky slopes that make a striking spectacle. In our younger days we frequently scrambled up some of its peaks, like Ger Tor, but today to follow the valley towards the confluence with the Rattle Brook was adequately tiring work. We stopped in the steepest part of the Cleave, sheltered from the strong wind, to enjoy a snack and absorb the atmospheric qualities of the gorge. It was so pleasant to be out of the violent wind that we elected to follow the Rattle Brook northwards to Bleak House using the Rattlebrook Hill/Hare Tor ridge as an effective windbreak. It was several degrees warmer in this lovely combe, a veritable sun trap even in November. The site of hut circles re-inforced the sheltered aspect of the Rattle Brook valley, a compensation for missing the views across the Tamar into Cornwall.

At Bleak House we took our lunch and indulged in a serious con-

versation about conservation. It was triggered by all the remains of former mining activities in the vicinity of Rattlebrook Head. The moor, in the last century, was heavily industrialized with men eking out a meagre living in dire conditions. Exeter businessmen funded the peat extracting enterprise whilst poor, generally uneducated men, worked throughout most seasons to make them, the business-men, rich. This led the conversation into politics, a great shame because Clive and I shared the same persuasions. It is difficult to get heated when you are in full agreement with someone. Thus, having solved half the world's problems, we walked between the Dunna Goats and up the gentle rise to the majestic Great Links Tor, high in our personal top ten of Dartmoor outcrops. Sadly it was again too windy to scramble up onto its summit. We headed south-westwards, the law of gravity responsible for our great speed.

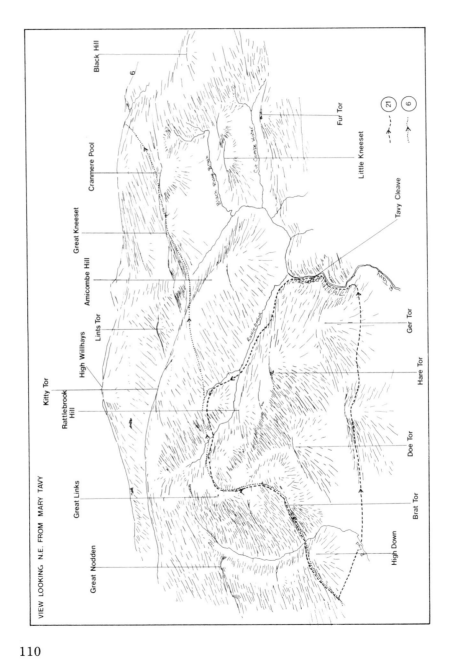

VIEW LOOKING N.E. FROM MARY TAVY

Black Hill
Cranmere Pool
Great Kneeset
Amicombe Hill
Lints Tor
High Willhays
Kitty Tor
Rattlebrook Hill
Great Links
Great Nodden

Fur Tor
Little Kneeset
Tavy Cleave
Ger Tor
Hare Tor
Doe Tor
Brat Tor
High Down

21
6

110

At Brat Tor we marvelled at the size of Widgery Cross, a fitting commemorative cross to the glorious reign of Queen Victoria on her Golden Jubilee in 1887. Mr. Widgery and his son were great local landscape artists who painted marvellous Dartmoor scenes. F.J. Widgery, who was also thrice Mayor of Exeter, had his Christian name initials adopted for Exeter car registrations. This and other gems of useless information kept us amused as we ran down from Brat Tor at an alarming and totally uncontrollable rate of knots. This time we crossed the Lyd via a small footbridge to complete our walk. We travelled back to Exeter via Tavistock, Princetown, Peking . . .

Dartmoor Letterboxes—Signed, Sealed and Discovered

There are more letterboxes on Dartmoor than there are tors, and there are about 180 tors! Hidden away in nooks and crannies, hidey holes, deep in creepy caves, high on lofty summits, embedded in dire mires and concealed in other exotic locations are hundreds of receptacles that bear a rubber stamp, and a visitors' book for those with a questing disposition to seek out. The last few years have seen a dramatic upsurge in this activity which has even spread to other kingdoms such as the far off peaks of Ascension Island.

Almost a century before Dartmoor received the restrictive or conservative status of National Park, James Perrot, a moorland guide from Chagford, demonstrated that he had a 'lot of bottle' by leaving one in the centre of a morass, on Northern Dartmoor, known as Cranmere Pool. This boggy hollow has acquired an immense reputation because many thousands of people have visited it since 1854. Calling cards and postcards are left for the next person to take on and post, whilst cryptic messages, ribald repartees, odd ditties and plain straightforward names and addresses are left in the visitors' book. The growth in the number of boxes from the genesis of Cranmere was slow. Belstone Tor had one from 1894 but the immense amount of rock there assured it of its semi-secrecy. Cranmere Pool, by comparison, was rudely on show and very much the Dartmoor bullseye, a target for walkers who often when reaching it are disillusioned at the lack of a pool and the grim miry surroundings.

Other locations attrated boxes, like Ducks' Pool, the Cranmere of Southern Dartmoor, a memorial to William Crossing who explored the moor more thoroughly than even the most ardent letterboxer, and often at the expense of an ear-bashing from members of his

family. His piratical spirit on the high seas of Southern Dartmoor's extensive swamps is preserved in memoriam with a simple inscription on a rock bordering the pool. Fur Tor, the professed Queen of Dartmoor's Tors, bears a long-established box owing to its remote spot so far from any metalled road that to reach it has deserved recognition.

Another original box was at Crow Tor, located in the beautiful West Dart Valley, to the north of Two Bridges. Sadly it has been a frequent victim of those intolerant folk who remove or defile letterboxes, either from sheer bloodymindedness or from staunch antibox beliefs. Almost all the boxes are well hidden and a great deal of thought has been put into their siting. At Ryder's Hill one walker actually sat on the letterbox for several minutes before realising it. The sensible self-imposed code of conduct which has been adhered to for the placement of boxes is as follows:

Boxes should *not* be situated:
1 In any kind of Antiquity, in or near stone rows or circles, cists or cairns, or in any kind of buildings, walls or ruins, peat cutters' or tinners' huts.
2 In any potentially dangerous situations where injuries could be caused. (Theoretically that would rule out the whole of Dartmoor in some circles!)
3 As a fixture, cement or any other building materials not to be used.

It is a great pity that letterboxers live in fear of some 'big brother' who might waspishly rule that only a handful of the original boxes shall remain. Such thoughts were aired in 1977 by the Dartmoor National Park resulting in the utmost of care being taken not to infringe on the DNP's apparent ideological philosophy for conserving the moor.

There appears to be a distinct two-faced appraisal of Dartmoor and what it is all about. In the Victorian era a great number of enterprises invaded Dartmoor to extract its mineral wealth. The miners and quarrymen, who populated the moor, disturbed its quietude and literally raped the scenery with ugly scars often on virgin territory. Such activity today would be more than frowned upon as even a single out of character signpost is scorned. However, these souvenirs of the golden age of legalised plundering are now held as hallowed industrial archaeological sites to be treated with managerial kid gloves.

The industrial past is well represented by letterboxes but do not expect to find the boxes easily at East Tinner's Heaps, Rubble Heap (Haytor), Haytor Railway, Wheal Emma Leat, Petre's Pits, London Pit, Red Lake, Blackaton Brook, Rattlebrook Peat Works, Bleak House, Statts House, Uncle Ab's House, Devonport Leat, Drake's Leat, Gibby Beam, Red Brook, Erme Pits, Knock Mine, Hooten Wheels, Hens Roost workings and so on. The boxes are often set away from the remains following the principles of the code of conduct. Many of the names only appear on the 2½ inch OS sheets of Dartmoor, a spin-off which must have the HMSO rubbing their hands in glee at the great number of committed walkers who dig deep into their pockets to enrich their locational knowledge of the moor.

Other themes which are developed by the 'boxers' include current affairs, e.g. the birth of the Royal baby, William, caused a temporary box to appear on Water Hill and the Falklands hostilities led to another at Manga Brook because of its supposed similarity to the Goose Green area.

Long forgotten legends have been rekindled in an illustrated fashion. Here you will see just one which shows Vixana the Witch on top of Vixen Tor. This 'foxy lady' has been remembered by a letterbox which will arouse interest in the legends and folklore of

Dartmoor. Other stories commemorated by aptly designed stamps and letterboxes include the legends of Bowerman's Nose (Vawr Maen), Grey Wethers, Cranmere Pool (Benjie), Childe the Hunter, the Tavistock Hare, the Gubbins and the Hairy Hands.

To reach the 'head' of a river is always regarded as an achievement, partly due to the inevitable climb and partly because the heads of rivers are often veritable quagmires where letterboxers like to wallow and entice others to struggle to reach their prize. All of these either have or have had boxes: Plym Head, Aune or Avon Head, Becky Head, Tavy Head, Cowsic Head, Strane Head, Teign Head, Smallbrook Head, Cholake Head, Yealm Head, East Dart Head and Walla Brook Head.

There are fun stamps like the ones of Chat Tor (a cat), Pork Hill (a pig) and Birch Tor. There are people remembered like Perrot, Crossing, Hansford Worth and Kathleen Parr, better known as Beatrice Chase, the Lady of the Moor. No doubt the eccentricities of this lady correspond favourably with the unusual behaviour of the boxers. There are even seasonal variations, Christmas, Easter and Halloween stamps. Many of the stamps' designs directly portray the object that appears in the name, e.g. Beardown and Fox Tor. Often the designs of these stamps are deliberately tongue-in-cheek but attractive enough to merit a safari into the gungiest of swamps or bogs to collect them.

Individuals who get the bug have their own personal stamps which have also become collectworthy items. Invariably instead of bearing the individual owner or groups real names, nicknames are adopted like Pixieled Perambulators, Rattery Peat Pounder, Mudlarks, Bogtrotters, Tormentors, Tor mites, Moor-ons and Room-trads.

Godfrey Swinscow is a man whose name is synonymous with letterboxing as it has developed into an all consuming hobby for him. He acts as the 'President' of a Dartmoor Letterbox Club, one which does not officially exist. A badge is awarded to walkers who prove they have visited 100 letterboxes, if they contact Mr Swinscow. To be a member of the '100 Club' is regarded as an achievement for many of the boxes demand map reading skills, detailed 1:25000 maps and possibly guidance from the Dartmoor Bible—Crossing's Guide. Because there are now so many boxes membership should be more easily attained.

A regular get together occurs twice a year at the Forest Inn, Hexworthy for the hundreds of letterbox enthusiasts. The dates of these meetings are easy to remember because they always co-incide with the changing of the clocks to or from British Summer Time. At these meetings 'members' exchange personal stamps, experiences and have a good time with folk of a similar disposition. Letterboxers have another venue at the Plume of Feathers in Princetown. Landlord, James Langton, has decorated part of the pub with his many stamps. He has testified that the letterbox fraternity comes from far afield. It is not uncommon for a weekend visitor to come from places like Aberdeen to search for biscuit tins buried in boggy hollows.

Letterboxing obviously engenders a common friendship bond amongst walkers keen to know and love Dartmoor, and if it encourages people of all ages to go out onto the moor with friends to enjoy themselves, then surely it is a good idea.

116

Near the "letterbox" on High Willhays—the highest point on Dartmoor.

Acknowledgements

And now that our boots have been hung up until the next moorland misadventure, all that remains to be done is to thank both the heroes and villains responsible for aiding and abetting us in this presentation. Our sincere thanks are due to: Dennis Johnston, Terry Bound, Tom Bolt, George Parsons, Dave Coombs, Paul Williams, Colin Kneeshaw, Mr Jones, Mr Youngson, the Phillips Family, Len Hunt, David Marsh, Darren Marsh, D.J. Hill.

Moor Places of Inn-terest!

The Old Inn at Widecombe

The Rugglestone Inn near Widecombe

The Sandy Park Inn near Chagford

The River Teign at Steps Bridge near Dunsford

119

OTHER OBELISK PUBLICATIONS

AROUND & ABOUT THE HALDON HILLS   Chips Barber

The Haldon Hills lie between the Exe Valley and Dartmoor. This book deals with almost every aspect of this 12 mile long hill range including geology, quarrying, railways, roads, walking, wildlife, and legends. There are also detailed studies of the towns and villages in and around these hills.

THE LOST CITY OF EXETER   Chips Barber

If you enjoy unusual anecdotes and would like to know the real Exeter—the villages within and without—its entertainment past and present, its sporting prowess and much more, you will love this lively book. It contains many illustrations including aerial views of the city.

THE TORBAY BOOK   Chips Barber

Did you hear about the smuggler who went to his own funeral? Or about the ghost who threw Beverley Nichols out of a window? Did you know that the toilets at Paignton Harbour were once a coastguard station or the ones on Torquay sea front were once an old toll house? Perhaps you may have been fooled by television and film makers who have used Torbay as the Mediterranean! The Torbay Book is packed with a vast number of strange tales and surprises from an area which includes Maidencombe, Babbacombe, St Marychurch, Torquay, Cockington, Paignton, Goodrington and Brixham.

ADVENTURE THROUGH RED DEVON   Raymond B Cattell

This is probably the finest book every written about the coastline, estuaries and rivers of South and East Devon. It is a warm, personal, and humorous account of journeys made through these areas between 1931 and 1935. There are detailed accounts of the history and unusual stories of all the places passed during these adventures. Ray Cattell gets marooned in Torbay, shipwrecked at Lyme Regis, encounters vicious swans, wicked weirs and obstinate locals on his voyage up the River Exe and spends a summer on a very different Dawlish Warren as it was in the 1930s. The "joys" of Newton Abbot station, the Teign's tidal race and beautiful girls all play their part in this book.

UNDER SAIL THROUGH SOUTH DEVON AND DARTMOOR
Raymond B Cattell

This is a continuation of "Red Devon" and deals with the South Devon coastline and its rivers which include the Dart, Avon, Erme, Tavy and Tamar. At the top of these rivers Ray forsakes his boat to explore the high moors. This is a wonderful adventure which will thoroughly entertain its readers.

AN EXETER BOYHOOD   Frank Retter

These tales are about childhood memories in Exeter. Frank tells of school life, markets, scouting adventures to green fields long gone, hardship and poverty. Illustrated by old and new photographs, and line drawings, it is a fascinating study of life at the turn of the century.

THE GREAT WALKS OF DARTMOOR   Terry Bound

This is the first book to include all the recognised long walks which take place on Dartmoor. It includes the Abbots Way, the North/South crossing, the Lich Way, the OATS walks, the Perambulation, the Dartmoor 100, the Ten Tors, the Mariners Way and the Tom Cobley walk. These walks are sufficiently detailed to enable a fit enthusiast to follow them.

IDE   Bill Rowland

This is the first book of our village series and is a colourful portrayal of life in a country village near Exeter from the turn of the century to the present day. It includes many entertaining and humorous anecdotes and gives a very good insight into the social conditions which prevailed in such an environment.

All titles available from **Obelisk Publications**, 2 Church Hill, Pinhoe, Exeter, Tel (0392) 68556.

Abbot's Way   88, 92
Abbot's Way, Alternative   95
Abbot's Way Walk Certificate   94
Addiscott   25, 27
Aish   59
Aish Tor   99, 100, 101
Amicombe Hill   31, 33, 110
Angler's Rest, Fingle Bridge   14, 16
Army Track   see Military Road
Arthur Clement   50, 52
Artillery Road   see Military Road
Aune   see Avon
Avon Dam Reservoir
                          43, 84, 86, 87, 90
Avon Head   84, 85
Avon Head Letterbox   115
Avon River   43, 45, 59, 86, 91
Avon Valley   90

Babeny   37, 81
Bag Tor   50, 53
Bagga Tor   40, 41
Bala Brook   43
Ball Gate   59
Ball Hill Quarry   71
Bay Tree   11
Beardown Farm   22
Beardown Hill   22
Beardown Letterbox   115
Beardown Tor   20, 22, 23
Beatrice Chase Letterbox   115
Becka Valley   77, 79
Becky Falls   79
Becky Head Letterbox   115
Bell Tor   52, 77
Bellever   37, 81, 82
Bellever Bridge   40
Bellever Forest   40
Bellever Tor   45, 46, 80, 82
Bellever Wood   79, 80
Belstone   9, 10, 11, 49, 69, 71
Belstone Renard   68
Belstone Ridge   69
Belstone Stocks   68
Belstone Tor   9
Belstone Tor Letterbox   111
Bench Tor   100, 101
Benjie Letterbox, Cranmere Pool 115
Bennet's Cross   29
Berry Head   50
Birch Tor   28
Birch Tor Letterbox   115

Bishop's Meads   43, 90, 92
Bittaford   42
Black Down   11, 41
Black Dunghill   23
Black Hill   53, 58, 110
Black Lane   85
Black Pool   44
Black Ridge Brook   110
Black Tor   7, 9
Black Tor Copse   7
Blackaton Brook   25, 27, 49
Blackaton Brook Letterbox   114
Black-a-Ven Brook   9, 69
Blackbrook River   73
Blackslade Down   52
Blackslade Mire   52
Bleak House   31, 32, 33, 108
Bleak House Letterbox   114
Bodmin Moor   31, 59, 94, 106
Boldventure   26
Bonehill Down   52
Bonehill Rocks   52
Bovey River   28, 53, 54
Bovey Tracey   53, 78, 79
Bovey Valley   55, 58
Bowerman's Nose   54, 78
Bowerman's Nose Letterbox   115
Brandis Cross   25, 27
Brat Tor   31, 33, 72, 110, 111
Bray, Reverend   22
Bridestowe   22
Broad Down   47
Broad Rock   90, 91
Broadun Ring   45, 47
Brockhill Ford   90
Brockhill Stream   84, 91
Brown Gelly   31
Brown Willy   31
Browsentor Farm   40
Buckfast Abbey   86, 88, 89, 91
Buckfastleigh   83, 86, 96, 101
Buckland Abbey   88
Buckland Beacon   50, 52
Buckland Common   50
Buckland Tor   53
Burford Down   60
Burrator Reservoir   17, 63, 67
Butterdon Hill   13, 43, 44, 45
Buttern Hill   103, 104

Castle Drogo   14, 35, 36
Castle Road   65, 92, 97

Cattell, Raymond   5, 87
Cawsand Hill   8, 9, 10, 25, 35, 78
Chagford
    13, 26, 32, 33, 34, 35, 103, 111
Chagford Common   27, 28, 29
Chalk Ford   96
Challacombe   28
Chat Tor Letterbox   115
Cherry Brook   38
Childe the Hunter   10
Childe the Hunter Letterbox   115
Chinkwell Tor   52, 53, 77, 78
Cholake Head Letterbox   115
Chudleigh, Elizabeth   60
Cleave, Derivation of   108
Cleave Hotel, Lustleigh   54, 55
Clement, Arthur   50, 52
Clifford Bridge   12, 16, 34, 35, 36
Clifford Cross   36
Cobley, Tom   24, 29, 52
Cocks Hill   40, 93
Cold East Cross   50
Coleridge Wood   12
Combeshead Farm   63
Combeshead Tor   63, 67
Combestone Tor   99, 100, 101, 102
Conies Down Tor   23
Coombe   14
Coombe Court   13
Corndon Tor
    28, 81, 82, 96, 99, 100, 101, 102
Cornwood   16
Corringdon Ball   43, 59
Cosdon   see Cawsand
Coursebeer   25
Cowsic Head   20, 22
Cowsic Head Letterbox   115
Cowsic River   20, 22, 40
Cox Tor   73, 93
Cranbrook   35
Cranbrook Castle   13
Cranmere Pool
        32, 33, 49, 70, 85, 110
Cranmere Pool Letterbox   32, 111
Crazywell Pool   65, 67
Cripdon Down   78
Criptor   72, 98
Crockernwell   11
Cross Furzes
    83, 84, 86, 87, 89, 90, 91, 92
Crossing Letterbox   115
Crossing, William   85, 94, 112

Crossing's Guide (Dartmoor Bible)
                                   115
Crossways   43, 45, 87, 90, 91, 92
Crow Tor   39, 40
Crow Tor Letterbox   113
Cuckoo Ball   59
Cuckoo Rock   17, 62, 64
Cuckoo Rock Letterbox   64
Cullever Steps   11, 45, 48, 69
Cut Combe Water   110
Cut Hill   23, 49

Dark Peak Fraternity   89
Dart Gorge   100
Dart River   86, 96, 99, 101, 108
Dart Valley Railway   96
Dartington Trust Woodlands   15
Dartmeet   80, 82, 99, 100, 102
Dartmeet Hill   101
Dartmoor Bible (Crossing's Guide)
                                   115
Dartmoor Inn, Bridestowe   22
Dartmoor Inn, Lydford   30, 33, 106
Dartmoor Inn, Merrivale
    see Merrivale Inn
Dartmoor Letterbox Club   115
Dartmoor Railway
    see Plymouth & Dartmoor Railway
Dartmoor Rescue Group   11, 12, 88
Dean Burn   86, 87, 90, 91
Dean Moor   92
Devil's Elbow   72, 75
Devil's Tor   20, 22, 23
Devonport Leat
            20, 61, 62, 63, 65, 66
Devonport Leat Letterbox   114
Dicky Pengelly   63
Dittsworthy Warren House   18
Doe Tor   110
Dogmarsh Bridge   14, 33
Dousland   64, 67
Down Ridge   46
Down Tor   67
Drake's Leat Letterbox   114
Drewsteignton   35
Duck's Pool   43, 83, 84, 85, 86
Duck's Pool Letterbox   112
Dunnagoats   31, 109
Dunsford   34, 35
Dunsford Woods   34

Easdon Tor   53, 78

ii

East Dart Head Letterbox 115
East Dart Hotel, Postbridge 46
East Dart River
    23, 38, 47, 80, 81, 82, 101, 103
East Hill 70
East Okement 9, 71
East Tinner's Heaps Letterbox 114
East Webburn River 28
East Webburn Valley 52
East Week 25
Eastern Tor 17, 18
Eddystone Light 60
Elizabeth Chudleigh 60
Ensworthy 102, 103, 104
Erme Pits Letterbox 114
Erme River
    43, 59, 84, 86, 87, 90, 91
Erme Valley 7, 44
Exeter 11, 42
Exeter, Mayor of 111
Exmoor 8
Eylesbarrow 17, 63
Eylesbarrow Down 67

Fatherford Viaduct 11, 71
Feather Tor 92, 93
Feather Tor Cross 94
Fernworthy 22, 26, 28, 35, 49
Fernworthy Forest 105
Fernworthy Reservoir 103
Fingle Bridge 14, 34, 35, 36
Fire Stone Cross 25, 27
Fish Lake 84, 85
Fish Lake Letterbox 85
Ford Park 26
Fordsland Lodge 7
Forest Inn, Hexworthy 46, 116
Fox Tor 44
Fox Tor 'By-Pass' 44
Fox Tor Letterbox 115
Foxtor Mire 44, 61, 62
Frenchbeer 26, 27
'Froggies in the Boggies' 68
Fur Tor 19, 20, 21, 22, 23, 49, 110
Fur Tor Letterbox 113

Gallaven Brook 104
Gallaven Mire 104
Ger Tor 108, 110
Gibby Beam Letterbox 114
Gidleigh 26, 27
Gidleigh Common 49, 104

Gidleigh Tor 26
Glaze Brook 43
Godfrey Swinscow 115
Gradner Rocks 79
Grant's Pot 84, 85
Grant's Pot Letterbox 85
Grea Tor 53, 76, 77
Greator Rocks 77
Great Gnats Head 17, 90
Great Kneeset 31, 33, 49, 110
Great Links 31, 110
Great Links Tor 33, 109
Great Mis Tor 73, 75, 93
Great Nodden 110
Green Hill 43, 85, 101
Green Tor 31
Greena Ball 75
Grey Wethers 105
Grey Wethers Letterbox 115
Grimspound 29
Gubbins Letterbox 115
Gutter Mire 18
Gutter Tor 17, 67

Hairy Hands Letterbox 115
Haldon Hills 84
Hall Farm 60
Halls Cleave 12
Hameldown 29, 77, 81
Hameldown Beacon 29
Hameldown Tor 28, 29
Hanger Down 60
Hangingstone 13
Hangingstone Hill 32, 33, 45, 48
Hare Tor 108, 110
Harford 43
Harry Price 14, 16
Hart Tor 67
Hartland Tor 48
Hartor Tors 17
Hay Tor 50, 53, 55, 75, 77, 98
Hay Tor 'By-Pass' 78
Haytor Down 58
Haytor Quarries 77
Haytor Railway 98
Haytor Railway Letterbox 114
Haytor Vale 53
Hayne Down 53, 54, 78
Headland Warren 29
Heckwood Tor 72
Hedge Barton 78
Hembury Fort 96

Hemerdon Ball   59
Hen Tor   18
Hen Tor Letterbox   18
Henlake Down   60
Hens Roost Workings Letterbox   114
Hew Down   32, 33, 104
Hexworthy   46
High Down   108, 110
High Willhays   7, 8, 9, 110
High Willhays Letterbox   117
Higher White Tor   20, 21, 23, 39
Hill Bridge   40, 41
Hillson's House   60
Hisley   55
Hockinstone Tor   100
Holne   86, 99, 101, 102
Holne Ram Roasting   46
Holne Ridge   99
Holy Brook   86
Holystreet Manor   33
Homerton Hill   7
Honeybag Tor   52, 54, 77
Hooten Wheels Letterbox   114
Hound Tor   10, 52, 53, 76, 77
Huccaby Bridge   46, 47
Huccaby Ring   80
Huccaby Tor   45, 46, 80, 101
Hunter's Path   14, 15, 34
Hunter's Tor   14, 53
Hunting Gate   14
Huntingdon Cross   91, 92
Huntingdon Warren   84, 86
Hurston   26
Hydro-electric Plant   40

Ingo Brake   41
Inns   see Pubs
Ivybridge   42, 43, 44, 60

James Langton   116
James Perrot   111
Jay's Grave   78
Jollylane Cott   45, 46
Jurston   26

Kathleen Parr   see Beatrice Chase
Kennon Hill   9, 49, 103
Kes Tor   26, 33, 49, 78, 103, 104
Kes Tor Inn, Manaton   54, 78
King Tor   28
King's Tor   73
Kingsett Down   41

Kingshead   29
Kingswear   50
Kitty Tor   110
Knock Mine Letterbox   114
Knowle   79

Lady of the Manor
   see Beatrice Chase
Lambs Down   87, 89, 90
Langton, James, Landlord of the
 Plume of Feathers, Princetown 116
Laughter Tor   80, 82
Leather Tor   63, 65, 67
Lee Moor   16
Leeden Tor   73, 93
Legis Tor   18
Leigh Bridge   33
Lemon River   50, 53
Letterboxes   111
Letterboxes, 100 Club   115
Letterboxes, Code of Conduct   113
Lich Way   22, 37
Lints Tor   110
Littaford Tors   20, 39
Little Haldon   50
Little Hound Tor   10
Little Kneeset   110
Little Wooston   12
Lizwell Meet   28
London Pit Letterbox   114
Long Ridge   105
Longford Tors   20, 22, 23, 39, 40
Longstone Hill   9, 11
Lower White Tor   39
Lud Gate   83, 84
Lustleigh   53, 54, 55, 56, 57, 58
Lustleigh Cleave   53, 54, 55
Lutyens   14
Lyd River   31, 33, 108, 111
Lydford   37, 41, 42
Lydford Gorge   42
Lydford Tor   20, 22, 23
Lydia Bridge   59
Lynch Common   18

Manaton   53, 54
Manga Brook Temporary Letterbox 114
Manga Hill   104
Mardle River   86, 91, 96
Mardon Down   13, 35
Mariners Way   26
Marsh Falls   47

iv

Mary Tavy   40, 110
Meavy River   17, 65, 67
Meavy Valley   66
Mel Tor   99, 100
Meldon   7, 9, 11
Meldon Hill   13
Meldon Reservoir   7, 11
Merrivale   21, 73, 74, 75, 92, 94
Merrivale Inn (Dartmoor Inn) 72, 74
Michelcombe   99, 101, 102
Military Road   8, 48, 69
Moor Brook   9
Moortown   92
Moortown Brook   27
Moreton - Newton Railway   79
Moretonhampstead   35, 55
Murray, Ruth   80

Naker's Hill   43, 101
Nat Tor   108
Natterdon Common   13
Nethercott   25, 27
Nethercott Farm   25
New Bridge   98, 99, 101, 102
Newton Abbot   55
North Hessary Tor   73, 91, 93, 94
North Teign River
                 27, 32, 33, 49, 103, 104
Northmoor   13
Northmoor Arms   26, 27
Nun's Cross   67
Nun's Cross Farm 44, 62, 90, 91, 92

O or Wo Brook   46, 100
Oke Tor   9, 45, 48, 49
Okehampton   9, 11, 42, 45, 48, 70
Okehampton Camp   9, 45, 48
Okehampton Castle   71
Okement Hill   9, 42, 49
Old Inn, Widecombe   118
Old Quarries   72, 73

Packsaddle Bridge, Bovey Valley
                                   58, 79
Peat Cot   92
Peek Hill   65
Pengelly, Dicky   63
Penn Beacon   16, 18
Perrot, James   111
Perrot Letterbox   115
Peter Tavy   93
Petertavy Great Common   75

Petertavy Inn   40
Petre's Cross   87
Petre's Pits Letterbox   114
Pew Tor   73, 93
Piddledown Common   14
Pil Tor   52
Piles Copse   7
Piles Hill   45
Pixie's Holt   80
Pixieland   80
Plume of Feathers, Princetown   116
Plym Head Letterbox   115
Plym River   18
Plymouth   60
Plymouth & Dartmoor Railway
                               72, 97, 98
Plymouth Library   32
Pondsworthy   28
Pork Hill Letterbox   115
Postbridge
  28, 38, 45, 46, 48, 79, 81, 82, 83
Powder Mills   23, 38, 39, 40
Prestonbury   36
Price, Harry   14, 16
Princetown   7, 18, 23, 60, 72, 73,
           80, 89, 90, 91, 92, 93, 97
Princetown Prison   90
Providence Place   26, 27
Pubs
  Angler's Rest, Fingle Bridge
                                   14, 16
  Cleave Hotel, Lustleigh   54, 55
  Dartmoor Inn, Bridestowe   22
  Dartmoor Inn, Lydford
                             30, 33, 106
  Dartmoor Inn, Merrivale   72, 74
  East Dart Hotel, Postbridge   46
  Forest Inn, Hexworthy   46, 116
  Kes Tor Inn, Manaton   54, 78
  Merrivale Inn   72, 74
  Northmoor Arms   26, 27
  Old Inn, Widecombe   118
  Petertavy Inn   40
  Plume of Feathers, Princetown
                                      116
  Ring o'Bells, Chagford   33
  Royal Oak, Meavy   16, 18, 19
  Rugglestone Inn, Widecombe   118
  Sandy Park Inn   14, 118
  Tom Cobley Tavern, Spreyton
                                   24, 25
  Tors Hotel, Belstone   11

Pubs (continued)
    Walkhampton Inn   64
    Warren House Inn
        28, 29, 102, 103, 105, 106
Pudsham Down   52
Puper's Hill   43, 83, 84, 86

Queen Victoria, Golden Jubilee 111
Quentin's Man   45, 48, 49, 103
Quickbeam Hill   45

Railways
    Dart Valley   96
    Haytor   98
    Moreton - Newton   76
    Plymouth & Dartmoor 72, 97, 98
    Red Lake Tramway   44, 84
Rattle Brook   33, 107, 108, 110
Rattlebrook Head   109
Rattlebrook Hill   108, 110
Rattlebrook Peat Works Letterbox
                      114
Raymond Cattell   5, 87
Red Brook Letterbox   114
Red Lake   43, 45, 86
Red Lake Letterbox   114
Red Lake Mire   90
Red Lake Tramway   44, 84
Red-a-Ven   9
Red-a-Ven Brook   11
Reddaford Leat   108
Refreshment Houses see Pubs
Richard Hansford Worth   44
Riddon Ridge   82
Ring o'Bells, Chagford   33
Ringmore Down   18
Rippa Tor (Rival Tor)   103, 104
Rippon Tor   50, 53, 96
Rival Tor see Rippa Tor
Rook   16
Rook Tor   16, 19
Roos Tor   73, 75, 93
Rough Tor   20, 23, 31
Row Tor   9, 11, 70
Royal Hill   44, 97
Royal Oak, Meavy   16, 18, 19
Rubble Heap Letterbox (Hay Tor) 114
Ruelake Pit   104
Rugglestone Inn, Widecombe 118
Rushford Farm   33
Rushford Mill   33
Ruth Murray   80

Ryder's Hill
    82, 86, 97, 99, 100, 101
Ryder's Hill Letterbox   113

Saddle Tor   50
St. Austell China Clay Pits 94
Sampford Spiney 72, 73, 93, 98
Sandy Hole Pass   47
Sandy Park   33, 35, 36
Sandy Park Inn   14, 118
Sandy Way   96, 99, 101
Satterley, Tom and Sally   46
Scarey Tor   9, 69
Scorhill   49
Scorriton   86, 95, 101
Scorriton Down   96
Shallowford   81
Sharp Tor
    14, 15, 36, 43, 99, 100, 101
Sharpitor   17, 67
Shaugh Prior   17
Sheeps Tor   17, 63, 64, 67
Sheepstor Village   64, 67
Shell Tor   17, 18
Shelstone Tor   7
Sherwell   81
Shovel Down   33, 104
Sig River   50, 53
Sigford   50
Silas Sleep   38
Simmons Park   70
Sittaford Tor   49, 103
Skir Hill   45, 46, 101
Sleep, Silas   38
Smallbrook Head Letterbox   115
Smallbrook Plains   87
Snowdon   43, 86, 96
Soussons Plantation   82
South Brent   59
South Hams   44, 50, 90
South Hessary Tor 67, 91, 92
South Teign River 26, 27, 103
South Zeal   102
Southbrook   79
Spitchwick   101
Spreyton   24, 25, 27
Stannon Tor   103
Staple Tors   73
Station Cat, Lustleigh 55, 56
Statts House Letterbox   114
Steeperton   8, 104
Steeperton Tor   9, 49

Steps Bridge
                30, 33, 34, 35, 36, 118
Stocks, Belstone   68
Stowford Mill   60
Strane Head Letterbox   115
Stringers Hill   85
Submarine (The)   see White Barrows
Swell Tor Quarries   72
Swincombe River   82, 97
Swinscow, Godfrey   115

Tavistock   18, 92, 93, 95, 98
Tavistock Abbey   88
Tavistock Golf Course   92, 95, 98
Tavistock Hare Letterbox   115
Tavistock
     Youth and Community College   88
Tavy Cleave
          6, 22, 106, 107, 108, 110
Tavy Head   20, 21, 22
Tavy Head Letterbox   115
Tavy River   40, 41, 92, 108, 110
Tavy Valley   98
Taw Head   33
Taw River   9, 45
Teign Estuary   50
Teign Gorge   13, 14, 15, 33
Teign Head Farm   105
Teign Head Letterbox   115
Teign River 14, 26, 33, 34, 35, 45
Teign Valley   12
Teigncombe   26, 27, 33
Ten Commandments Stones 50, 51, 52
Ter Hill   46, 62, 86, 97, 101
Thornworthy   26
Thornworthy Tor   103
Three Barrows   45, 59
Throwleigh   25, 26, 27, 102, 103
Tom Cobley   24, 29, 52
Tom Cobley Tavern, Spreyton   24, 25
Tom Satterley (and Sally)   46
Top Tor   52, 53
Tor Royal   97
Torbay   50
Torquay   50
Tors Hotel, Belstone   11
Totnes   50
Trendlebere Down   58
Trowlesworthy Tors   17, 18
Two Bridges 7, 20, 22, 23, 44, 113

Ugborough Beacon   43

Ugborough Moor   59
Uncle Ab's House Letterbox   114
Uppacott Down   13
Upper Plym River   67
Upper Plym Valley   91

Vawr Maen   see Bowerman's Nose
Venford Reservoir   82, 99, 101
Vixana   74, 75
Vixen Tor   74, 94
Vixen Tor Letterbox   114
Vixen Tor Mire   74

Walkham River
   40, 64, 72, 73, 75, 92, 93, 94, 98
Walkhampton   60, 64, 65, 67
Walkhampton Church   64, 65
Walkhampton Inn   64
Walla Brook
           33, 49, 81, 82, 103, 104
Walla Brook Head Letterbox   115
Ward Bridge   72, 73, 98
Warren House Inn
           28, 29, 102, 103, 105, 106
Watchet Hill   69
Water   54
Water Hill   103
Water Hill Temporary Letterbox   114
Water Oak Corner   91
Waterfall   45
Watern Tor   13, 32, 49, 104
Watervale   41
West Dart River
            20, 22, 23, 39, 40, 101
West Dart Valley   113
West Mill Tor   9, 10, 70
West Okement River   7, 32, 49
West Webburn River   28, 77
Western Beacon   43, 44, 45
Wheal Emma Leat Letterbox   114
Whiddon Down   35
Whiddon Park   14, 15, 34
Whiddon Woods   13
Whitchurch Down   92, 95, 98
White Barrows (The Submarine)
                40, 84, 86, 87
White Hill   108
White Ridge   103, 106
White Tor   93
Whitehorse Hill   48, 103
Whiteworks   60, 62, 67
Whiteworks Mire   61

Whitley, Mr.   50
Widecombe-in-the-Moor
        24, 28, 29, 30, 37, 52, 77
Widecombe Fair   24
Widgery, F.J.   111
Widgery Cross, Brat Tor 31, 72, 111
Wild Tor   13, 49, 103, 104
William Crossing   85, 94, 112
Willingstone Rock   13
Willsworthy Camp   41
Willsworthy Down   41
Wind Tor   28
Winneys Down   45, 48
Wistman's Wood   7, 20, 23, 39
Wonson   26

Wooston   12, 36
Wooston Castle   16
Worth, Richard Hansford   44

Y.H.A.   26, 27
Yar Tor   80, 82, 99, 100, 101, 102
Yardworthy   26, 27
Yarner Wood   53
Yealm Head Letterbox   115
Yealm River   18
Yellowmead Down   64
Yelverton   67
Yennadon Down   64
Yes Tor   9, 10, 70

Zoar   40, 41